Property Management
By
Scott Bolinger
5th Edition

**A detailed guide In Property Management, Property
Preservation and Property Inspections**

WR Publishing
http://bolinger-and-associates.com/property-management-book.html
www.WarriorRage.com

Also by Scott Bolinger

1 of 3
Boxing Basics Level 1

2 of 3
Boxing Basics Level 2

3 of 3
Boxing Basic 3 & 4

Masters Edition
WarriorRage KickBoxing

Volume I
WarriorRage KickBoxing

Volume II
WarriorRage KickBoxing

Standalone
Officials Training Book for Combat Sports
Weight Lifting
Stretching by Scott Bolinger
National Self-Defense Solutions
Property Management by Scott Bolinger
Bolinger KickBoxing
Politics: Last Act of Defiance

Watch for more at larrybolinger.com/index.html.

Disclaimer

The publisher and author of this book are not responsible in any manner whatsoever for any income loss. What is stated are several ideas that have worked in creating income. Sometimes it takes money to make money.

Published by:

Scott Bolinger
Address: 507 Niobrara
Alliance, NE 69301
Phone: 308-760-7346 Email: LB@LarryBolinger.com
Website: www.LarryBolinger.com[1]
Website: www.WarriorRage.com[2]
Revised December 2013
Revised April 2014
Revised 2018
Revised 2020
Revised 2022

---

1. http://www.LarryBolinger.com

2. http://www.WarriorRage.com

About the Author

Scott Bolinger has been a business owner for over 15 years, and has been investing in investment properties for over 10 years, and started in preservation work and field inspections in 2006. He has a background in Carpentry, locksmith, and masonry that started in the AirForce in 1987. The property investment went from starting from scratch to over $500,000 worth of investment property. Is the author of several books, business books, martial arts books, self-defense books, and history and 2018 Congressional candidate from Nebraska.

Introduction

I'd guess since you decided to buy a copy of this book that you're a business-minded person that wants to get straight to the point and create an additional cash flow. There are several ways to create income in property management. The business I'll be going through is as a Contract Inspector and there are many aspects of a contract inspector that covers field inspections, property verifications, merchant site inspections, and preservation which consists of contract work with asset companies to bring the foreclosed property up to FHA/HUD regulations, and some standard tidbits of property management. You don't have to do everything, but I find it best to diversify your income. The companies you would be working with are contracting companies that work with mortgage companies or realty brokers, asset companies, and banks and in some cases, you might work directly with the mortgage company. Primarily what a field inspector would do is perform property verifications. This would have you going out to a property and verifying that someone still lives at the property in which you would take one picture of the front of the house, maybe a picture of the address and down the street, or to do interior and exterior property inspection of a property that isn't occupied and you would take pictures on all sides of the outside of the building and two pictures per room and place bids on anything that makes the building non-compliant (not up to FHA code). For the preservation work, you would make sure that the building is secured and complies with FHA guidelines. For the Preservation work you would take pictures of all sides of the house, then 2 pictures per room in the interior. You're usually given a list of tasks and you would take before, during, and after pictures of work that was approved to be completed. For preservation work you would be primarily doing winterizations, securing a property, yard work, maid service, disposal of hazardous material...etc. Sometimes the preservation work isn't just limited to FHA guidelines, sometimes the mortgage companies, realtors, or asset companies may have general remodeling that they want to be done, or maybe the city building inspector may have written up work that's needed doing, which would get approved through an asset company.

Content

Personal Property Notice

Chapter 1
Intro To Property Preservation

In property preservation, there are 3 primary areas for work. Inspections, Property Preservation, REO. The inspector or field inspector will do a general inspection of the property. Either just an outside inspection to do a property verification or occupancy verification to see if someone still lives at the property or if it's been abandoned. Along with the field inspector side of that business is the interior/exterior inspection. When you do an interior/exterior inspection you are mainly looking to see if the place is still secured and in compliance. You would check to see if there are any safety hazards, roof leaks, or water leaks that could cause more harm to the property, and you point out any issues of vandalism. Some inspections could be insurance loss inspections. That type of inspection is when a homeowner received damages to their home from a storm. You would do the inspection and verify the completed work. Some inspections may be to inspect a business. Most business inspections are to verify its existence to help that business get approved for a credit card reader. And then there is the maintenance part of the preservation which would be to secure a property, winterize, yard maintenance, maid service, and bring a house up to FHA code. On the first interior / exterior inspections you want to do a very thorough inspection of the property. If you're not approved to do the work, then you make bids to do the work. Some prices are pretty standard. Like lock changes, installing a lockbox, installing hasp and lock, dry winterization. But some things may have some flexibility like debris removal, initial yard maintenance, and maid service. So in certain circumstances, you might consider one bid set out with separate prices with the total, then a total bid as a bundle package with a discount for the packaged deal. I do have a standard list price in this book, I wouldn't go much out of that range. I would not recommend bidding lower than the prices I provide. Things you'll have to consider when doing your bid, are travel, material expense, and room and board if you have to stay out of town for 2 or 3 days and the percentage the asset company is going to take. So if they are taking 20%, then add an extra 20% to your bid. If they are going to take 50%, then double your bid price. There are two areas of the foreclosure process. One is the pre-foreclosure. In a pre-foreclosure, a contractor can only sure one door, do limited work, and do a report. In a pre-foreclosure, a mortgagor can reclaim that property. This property is assumed abandoned before any work is completed. The property is verified abandoned by the inspectors. After the property is sold or acquired by the bank, then it is considered foreclosed. The bank has all rights to the property. Then they will make the order for a full cleanout with a list of allowable jobs that could be done to the property to bring it up to FHA code.

Definitions

Drive-by inspections (property verification or Occupancy Inspection): this type of inspection is done to see if someone is still living at the property. And you take one picture of the front of the house, one of the address, and a picture showing down the street and street sign. A lot of companies want you to take double pictures, which is good practice. It decreases the chance of a blurry photo. The form you get for this type of inspection will generally ask for a description of the house which would cover type and color of siding, type of covering on the roof, estimate value of the property, visible personal property, any broken or boarded up windows or doors. If the property is vacant then you would usually do a full exterior set of photos (all 4 sides of the house, down the street, street sign, address, gas meter, electric meter), and sometimes the inspection would require to check with a neighbor to confirm that it's occupied or not. In some cases, if it's vacant then you would post a vacancy sticker on the window.

Interior/Exterior inspection: Take pictures of the outside and all for sides of the house, down the street, pic of the gas meter and electric meter, roof pics, and then take two pictures of every room, and picture of the ceiling and floor of each room, pic of the water heater, furnace, and water meter. Jot down any issue that would be needed to bring the property up to compliance (securing property, boarding windows or doors, removal of hazardous materials, property inspections, any safety hazards, trip hazards, rails needed on the stairway, yard maintenance)

Merchant site inspections: this would be an inspection on a business to make sure it's legitimate. This is usually a by appointment inspection. Usually consist of 5 exteriors and 5 interior pictures, making sure you take a picture of all 4 sides of the exterior of the building and pictures of the sign. In the interior, you'll usually need to take pictures of the general business area, main office, picture of where secured documents are kept (usually a file cabinet), and inventory. A lot of times you're there to qualify a company to use or continue the use of credit cards readers, so you'll take pictures of the credit card machine. The inspection is to check to make sure the business is legitimate. I've had several for auto sales to qualify them to be able to contract with a company that does background checks so that they can set up the loans themselves.

Inventory inspections: inspection of inventory, taking pictures, and writing down serial numbers to confirm the correct item. Inventory inspections would be done on stores or restaurants. It is usually about a $300 job.

Insurance Loss Inspections: inspection of a building that has had weather damage. Usually take an average of 30 pictures. Collateral inspections, rush inspections, construction site inspections, occupancy inspections, commercial inspections, and delinquency inspections. Out in Nebraska, I get a lot of inspections for hail damage, and the most common is roof repair, siding, gutters, and down spouts. You'll take pictures of completed work and work that still needs to be done and whether or not there satisfied with the work that has been completed.

Collateral inspections: this would usually be for construction equipment that someone has rented. The last one I did was an excavator. You'll need to take several pictures at a distance and several up-close pictures of all sides of the equipment and the serial number.

Rush inspections: a rush inspection could be any of these types of inspections but you'll generally have 48 hours to complete. But you'll charge a higher price for the limited time frame

Construction site inspection: This may be a few different things, maybe a percentage of completion on a job, or an equipment inventory.

Occupancy inspections: same as a drive-by inspection. This is just to verify occupancy

Commercial inspections: this could be to verify the legitimacy of the business just like the merchant site inspection or inventory inspection

Delinquency inspections: these are usually on vehicles and you would generally take pictures of all sides of the vehicle and the VIN number and do an interview

Preservation and REO: generally when called on this type of inspection, it may be assigned as a preservation work order. This could be on an abandoned house that went back to the mortgage company, reversed mortgage, or foreclosed property, or a property that a broker bought and contracted you to do an initial. An initial would be a first-time clean, yard maintenance, secure, debris removal, winterization if in season. So you would go in and secure the house. Change the locks to a specific key code and secure any outbuildings (garage, shed), secure any pools or hot tubes, and install a lockbox if the work order has that listed. Depending on what time of year it is, you may be required to winterize a property by disconnecting pipes at the water heater, disconnecting the water meter, blowing out the lines, capping the feed line, cleaning the toilets, pressure testing the lines, then poor RV anti-freeze in each drain. Some work orders may approve fixing roof leaks, removal of debris, maid service, yard service boarding windows, doors, pet doors. You may have just a couple of things approved, then you'll have to write up bids for everything else to bring the property into compliance.

Camera

When purchasing a camera a few tips you'll need to know. You'll need a digital camera. When buying a camera try and get more than one battery. It's good to have more than one camera. You never know when a battery or camera will go out on you. And if you get a camera that uses AA or AAA batteries, I suggest getting rechargeable batteries and a charger. Those types of batteries hold a charge a lot longer. After you purchase a camera, set the date, then set your picture pixel to 640 which is probably your lowest setting. If you are unable to set your pixels you can download a free photo resizer at:

www.faststone.org/FSResizerDetail.htm[1]

http://www.reaconverter.com/resize-images.html?gclid=CKHdjKXelqkCFZQbKgod8VB6uA

http://getgimp.com/lp/index.php?pid=TR&s=google&c=getgimp&pk=279&country=US&brand=

http://www.mystikmedia.com/photo_resizer_software.htm

If you have a cell phone that takes good pictures, that can be acceptable. But doing pictures with a cell phone, you might have to load the pictures into your computer and resize them to 640 x 480 with the photo resizer. I'd suggest the FastStone resizer. Then you'll have to add a date and time stamp to each picture. I would suggest going to www.watermark-software.com[2] , that's a very simple program that can crop, date, and time stamp, and group pictures at one time. Some companies may have an android application, so you can take pictures and auto-download to their website directly to the work order. Some companies may also want a picture of longitude and latitudes. So a GPS app might need to be down load.

Here is a list of companies that I work with regularly. The main thing, if you're looking at making inspections a full-time business, you'll need to spend a couple of days sending resumes to as many companies as you can. Sending out one resume and expecting to get work immediately won't cut it. Send out 30 to 100, and then you should see some activity.

---

1.   http://www.faststone.org/FSResizerDetail.htm

2.   http://www.watermark-software.com

Field Service Companies

http://www.sandcastlefs.com/

MSI : https://enterprise.msionline.com/login.aspx?enc=HAd1rtUZbsmBBo0sEDuy4YEaENNjZLnGBtpfRZdjcl

http://www.fivebrms.com/

www.fiveonline.com[3]

http://www.fieldservices.com/

https://secure.nvms.com/application/Default.aspx

http://www.a2zfieldservices.com/

National Field Services

http://inspector.complytraq.com/Inspect/Inspect.dll

https://contractors.gcsresearch.com/

http://www.parrinspections.com/pw/public/index.aspx

http://www.pbdisasterservices.com/inspectors/inspector_registration.aspx

https://vnet.safeguardproperties.com/Login.aspx

Altisource

Guardian Asset Management

National Field Representatives

websites with lists of field service companies

the business portal.com: http://www.thebusinessportal.com/subpage.asp?node=206261&CTitle=Field_Service_Companies&Loc=%5(

http://www.spiritsearch.com/finance_field_service_companies.shtml

In a search engine type in some keywords that should bring up some sites to send applications to. Look for field inspector, preservation, mortgage field services. For most of the sites, you shouldn't have to send them money to sign up with them.

Paid sites:

https://global-data-entry.com/Data_Entry_Jobs.html : this is actually the first online information that I bought into. I had it saved

---

in my email for probably a year or two, then fumbled back through my saved emails and figured I'd give it a shot. It gave me a pretty good start in the field inspections business. It provided me with several ideas on different database businesses with several ways on how to market online, selling ebooks, field services, and much more. The information on marketing to any salesperson is priceless.

http://www.sofi.us/home_page.html: I highly recommend this site and book. I bought this a couple of years ago and it helped me get a few companies to contract with and my field service is listed with them and I've received several calls because of my listing with them. I quickly made back the money I spent. There is also www.sofiblog.com[4] and Facebook at https://www.facebook.com/SOFINetwork#%21/pages/SOFI-Networking/112269105499705?v=wall&ref=ts[5]

Facebook groups:

https://www.facebook.com/property.preservation.14/
https://www.facebook.com/groups/581608701940011/
https://www.facebook.com/propertypreservationprocessors/
https://www.facebook.com/propertyprespro/
https://www.facebook.com/propertypreservationservicing/
https://www.facebook.com/groups/propprez/
https://www.facebook.com/groups/PPContractors/
https://www.facebook.com/groups/1522095354744926/
https://www.facebook.com/groups/558527394215498/

---

4.   http://www.sofiblog.com

5.   https://www.facebook.com/
SOFINetwork#_0bcef9c45bd8a48eda1b26eb0c61c869_21_6666cd76f96956469e7be39d750c
c7d9_pages_6666cd76f96956469e7be39d750cc7d9_SOFI-Networking_6666cd76f96956469e
7be39d750cc7d9_112269105499705_d1457b72c3fb323a2671125aef3eab5d_v_43ec3e5dee6e
706af7766fffea512721_wall_6cff047854f19ac2aa52aac51bf3af4a_ref_43ec3e5dee6e706af7766
fffea512721_ts

Business info sites:

Any field and preservation company will have specific rules to follow. They have to follow HIPPA, FHA, and HUD guidelines. Brush up on these rules regularly. A bit of good advice, if a company says to do something that isn't within those guidelines I would question it or don't work for that company.

HUD

http://www.hud.gov/offices/oig/careers/

HUD inspection training: http://portal.hud.gov/hudportal/HUD?src=/program_offices/public_indian_housing/reac/products/pass/pass_trng

HIPPA

http://www.hipaa.com/

Mortgage field rep community (good for tips): http://mortgagefieldrep.ning.com/main/authorization/signIn?target=http%3A%2F%2Fmortgagefieldrep.ning.com%2F%3Fxg_so

http://cubicyard.us/ : this is a very helpful site. It has a great deal of information about rules and regulations. Some inspection companies require you to sign up with this site. Not many, but some, and it does have a lot of good information.

Video training: http://www2.safeguardproperties.com/pop/?p[0]=3&p[1]=Reverify+Convey+Condition&p[2]=vc09/day2session3.flv&p[3]=2560&p[4]=266&p[5]=4242[6]

Supply company:

http://www.mfssupply.com/

Quality Control and Processing: If you need help in managing your business and have a crew looking over all your crew's work could help generate a lot more jobs and a significant increase in the amount of money you make. I would recommend Benchmark Preservation

---

6.   http://www2.safeguardproperties.com/

pop/?p%5B0%5D=3&p%5B1%5D=Reverify+Convey+Condition&p%5B2%5D=vc09/

day2session3.flv&p%5B3%5D=2560&p%5B4%5D=266&p%5B5%5D=4242

at http://benchmarkpreservations.com/. I did Quality Control work with this bunch for a while.

Lock Pick tinplates for Preservation workers. Takes a lot of practice to use picks. Most times it's just best to drill out a lock and save yourself some time. I'd invest in a good battery drill that comes with two batteries. A pipe wrench may work on opening knoblocks as well.

http://www.lockpickguide.com/lockpicktemplates.html

helpful links:

longitude and latitude map

http://universimmedia.pagesperso-orange.fr/geo/loc.htm

Business Management

The property preservations business can be a wide selection of work. Where you contract with different banks, asset companies, companies that contract with asset companies, realty agents, and brokers. And they'll give you a work order that maybe what they would call an "initial service". Which could cover lawn service, maid service, secure, winterization, and debris removal.

With the preservation department, you can create a significant income off just preservation work. But, you can also put some focus on individual departments. I told people for many years, that you can make good money just off yard care. You can do a little advertising just for yard maintenance and get your clientele up. As a kid taking care of lawns you might make 10 bucks here 10 bucks there, but as a business, you can't rely on possible business that may occur. So when you get your clients, you set up reoccurring lawn serves. You get your client, then you set the date at every 10 to 14 days, so they don't have to call you, and then you send them a bill. You already have your date set, and you usually run with that from May to October. Going from your standard preservation work in the winter, spring and then moving to summer and adding yard service could mean an extra 2 to 3k a month. I worked in a regional area which is about a 100-mile radius from where I live. I took care of roughly 80 properties in the region. If your lawn care department gets some commercial property, that could be some good bonus money.

When buying equipment, you should buy equipment that can handle the workload. The first year I ran a yard service, some riding mowers lasted a month, some maybe 2 months, I went through 3 push mowers and a couple of weed eaters. That can add up. On riding a mower, you're best to go with a commercial-grade mower. The zero turns are great. They have good power, the transmission doesn't slip, and you get the job done a lot faster than on a standard riding mower.

I would strongly recommend not going with a riding mower that has a friction disk transmission. Those won't last long. If you have a riding mower, always take a push mower just in case. You don't want to be in a situation where you're out in the boonies and the riding mower breaks and you are left with just a weed eater to mow a lawn with. What I usually take with me on a Yard Maintenance job is a riding mower, push more, 2 weed eaters, a leaf blower, and some tree limb saws and snips, a chain saw, gas, 2 cycle oil, weed eater string, tire pump, and some standard tools. You don't have to start with this much stuff, but the object is to get the job done quickly and move on to the next job. The more jobs that are done, the more money.

On the maid service or janitor service, this could be singled out as well. You have your standard preservation maid service clients, then you can expand on that. Maybe get contracts from old folks' homes. Sometimes retired people may want weekly or monthly maid service or handy capped people. With a little advertising, you can expand this quite a bit. Put out some fliers, or newspaper advertisements, or advertise through the chamber of commerce, but always have business cards handy. The newspaper ads can be expensive. I might budget maybe once a year on newspaper ads. You should always set up some sort of time frame where you focus on advertisement. You will always gain and lose business. Setting up different months to send out some standard advertisements will help to decrease low months. Most of my business comes from word of mouth. A lot of times the word of mouth comes from realtors that I do business with. So sending out fliers to realtors of your maid service may kick in some extra business. I've found extra business on Facebook and craigslist. A lot of cities have garage sell channels and people post jobs on there. A good way to snag up some extra business. The one-time client is fine, but it's best to get a reoccurring client. Set up a service maybe once a week, every two weeks, or once a month. You may be able to stir up some extra clients by working with case workers that manage the elderly or subcontract with HUD or contract with a broker.

On getting paid. There is a lot of ways to do that. The main thing is to have the ability to give your clients options. You send a bill and have them pay once a month, pay cash while you're on the job, or set up a website and set up pay it now buttons for services and they pay through Paypal or credit card. With a Paypal account payments may be done with Paypal, or credit card as a member or guess. Or you can get a square, where you plug in a device into your cell phone and you can accept a credit card payment on the spot. Giving more options on how to pay, helps your clients. And it helps so you don't end up with an overload of accounts receivables. Accounts receivables would be money that people owe you. A few hundred in accounts receivables isn't too bad, but several thousand can be a drain on a business. Especially if you are having to manage some of your business on credit cards, accounts, or have workers to pay.

You may want to set up several accounts at hardware stores, a credit card for business, maybe a home depot and/or Menards account or other lumber yards, maybe get a gas account. But only use these in emergencies. You'll have to manage these well and don't charge more than you can financially handle. At lumber yards, you can set up a regular account or a contractor's account. If you are doing a lot of remodeling, I'd try and get a contractor's account. Sometimes you can get discounts or specials.

It would probably be a good idea to create your business name and get a banking account under your business name. and possibly create an LLC. There are more tax incentives as an LLC. You can get by with a sole proprietorship but you just don't get enough tax incentives. Forming an LLC, you can create your board, hire yourself and your significant other.

In contracting with the different companies, they will most likely require you to fill out a W9, maybe get a background check, you may have to pay for your background check, there may be a lengthy questionnaire. You may be required to carry liability insurance. If you're doing just inspections, you may not be required to carry insurance. But some require liability insurance, or both liability and E&O insurance. Some may require a contractor's license. For a contractor's license, you would need just a general contractor's license, and you get that through the city municipality. It might cost $50 to $75 to get, and you may need to show proof of insurance.

Insurance

At the minimum, you would want to have general liability insurance or handyman insurance. If you are just doing inspections, some companies don't require insurance. If you're doing Property Preservation work, most companies will require that you carry 1 million in liability insurance. Usually, just a general contractor or handyman liability insurance will do. Some companies might require that you have Errors and Omission insurance. But usually, you can negotiate around that. General liability insurance may run between $600 to $1400, and that may depend on what there covering for. Doing roof repair, working on structural, demo, hazardous waste control, mold removal, asbestos removal may increase the cost of liability insurance. So if you're not going to do those hazardous jobs, then don't have them on your insurance. Or subcontract those types of jobs out and take a 20% commission. E&O insurance usually runs around $2500. A lot of companies will require it, but if you really can't afford it, then see if you can get around that. But if you're a realtor or broker, then there is no way around it.

If you can't afford even liability insurance. You can try and find a company or contractor that will umbrella you under their business. Usually, what happens there, they can create a department for your business, or extend their coverage area, and whatever work that's created, they'll usually deduct 20% off the top to umbrella you. 20% off the top is pretty standard.

Contractor's License

On licensing. It would be a good idea to get a general contractor or handyman license. You get that through the cities municipality. Probably at your building and zoning department. But, you'll need your liability insurance before you go there. And in some cases, the license goes up in front of the city council for approval. Could take a month to get your card. But, that shouldn't stop you from getting work done. Several companies like to see their contractors with licenses and it's a good way to get extra work. After you get your local license, the state might require you to register with them as well.

Here is an example of a resume for field inspection or preservation work. This is the first thing you should set up. Use this form to help you get started.

RESUME
(Field Inspector and Preservation)

Name: Scott Bolinger

    Company: Bolinger & Associates

    Address:

    City/State/Zip:

    Phone:

    Fax:

    Email:

    Website: www.Bolinger-and-Associates.com[1]

Experience:

Bolinger and Associates have been in business since 1998 and expanded into property management in 2001 and into field inspections and preservation in 2007. We are one of the leading inspection/preservation companies in Western Nebraska. We are working on expanding to carry a larger workload. We do have the equipment to handle most preservation or REO work orders (digital camera, computer, internet access, printer, and fax machine, lawn service equipment, plumbing tools, general handyman tools, generator, boarding tools, and supplies, cleaning supplies .... Etc

Types of Inspections we will do:

Drive-by inspections, interior, and exterior house inspections, Quality Control Inspections, merchant site inspections, inventory inspections, insurance inspections, collateral inspections, rush inspections, construction site inspections, occupancy inspections, commercial inspections, delinquency inspections, preservation, and REO. We may expand our types of inspection and areas we work with depending on the demand outside our region. We are also equipped to be able to do some remodeling and painting work.

The zip codes I we cover:

69301, 69341, 69334, 69336, 69361, 69348,69337, 69339, 69347, 69360, 39343, 69357, 69131

County Coverage:

Box Butte, Morrill, Sheridan, Dawes, Scottsbluff, Sioux, Garden, Cheyenne

Note: may except quotes for going outside of areas.

---

1.   http://www.Bolinger-and-Associates.com

Price List

Some companies will require you to set your own price but most will already have their standard cost. You as an independent contractor you will have to accept or decline their price or do a counter bid. Below is a pretty standard price list. Depending on the travel, you might want to tack on a trip charge. The standard is between 50 cents to one dollar per mile for a trip charge.

Property Preservation Type	Price
Hazards	
Cleaning Refrigerators or cleaning a stand-alone freezer	$75
Clean toilet	$75
Capping Wires	$3 each
Capping Water main	$10 each
Removing gas can(s) or propane tank(s)	$15 each
Tire removal	$10 each
Mold removal	Open bid
Remove water from the basement	Open bid
Replace sump pump	Open bid
Remove carpet and dry wall from a flooded basement	Open bid
Install rail (3 or more steps)	$7 per foot
Install Smoke Detector	$25 each
Install carbon dioxide detector	$45 each
Roof repair	
Patch or re-shingle (standard price with low pitch)	$245 per square
Tarp 10 x 20 sq ft area	$400
Boarding	
Windows	75 UI or less $70 76 – 100 UI $90 101 – 125 UI $115
Slider door or single garage door	$160
Double garage door	$175
Security door	$250
Crawl space or pet door	$60

Lock changes and securing

	$60 for the first lock
Knoblock and deadbolt change	$40 for every lock after that
Padlock	
Padlock and hasp	$20 each
Window Lock	$20 each
Slider lock	$20 each
LockBox	$20

Lawn Maintenance

Initial Lawn Cut (up to 10,000 sq ft)	$100
Initial Lawn Cut (10,001 to 15,000 sq. ft)	$150
Initial Lawn Cut (over 15,000 sq. ft)	Open bid
Re-cut (up to 5000 sq. ft)	$40
Re-cut (5001 to 10,000 sq. ft)	$65
Re-cut (10,001 to 15000 sz.ft)	$ 85
Re-cut (over 15001 sq. ft)	Open Bid
Trim Shrubs	$35

Winterize

Snow Removal (standard sized property)80 feet of sidewalk and 20 X 40 feet of drive way) May negotiate for over sized area or commercial property	$75
Winterization for Dry winterization	$125
Defrost frozen pipes (minimum 8 hours) for one unit of no more than one water heater and no more than 3 bathrooms	$500

Debris Removal

Exterior and interior debris removal	$32 cyrds

Personal property removal and storage	$32 cyrds for removal $50 for a storage unit for one month

Miscellaneous (for any works not listed)
Rental Property Management

Rental Property management	20% of total rent

Maid Service

The standard for a first-time maid service	$150
Maid Refresh	$55

Direct Contracts: On a direct contract with a bank and broker, I would try and establish a standard allowable. Some companies run a $1500 allowable, some are at $2500. That gives you enough, for when you get an initial service, that you can go in and do the winterization, yard maintenance, 35 cyrds of debris removal, maid service, and emergency repairs. And you'll need to establish what can be considered emergency repairs. Roof leaks are usually emergency repairs, some companies would want you to tarp a roof, some companies want you to do a permanent fix. Push for approvals for covers for receptacles and light switches, wire nuts on bare wires, rails for stairs that have 3 or more steps, fix broken steps, plumbing repair/leaks, add a smoke detector on each floor, paint over graffiti, boarding, glazing windows, securing. I'd try and push for when you do an initial that everything gets secured (house, garage, shed any outbuilding). The thing with having an allowable is setting it up so you know what you can automatically do, and just get it done, then submit the invoice. That way you don't have to put in bids on everything and make an extra trip to get the work done.

Creating a contract directly with a bank will usually consist of working with a broker to manage the process.

Bundle: On a bundled bid, what you would set up with a company that you contract with is standard pricing for a group of work tasks. The total in the bundle would be your initial. This work and price would be set and approved for every initial work order without asking for approval for each work order. With this, you might make more or make less. Where most work orders may have between 5 and 10 cyrds, you'll come out quite a bit ahead. When it's around 20 cyrds, you are still making money, just not quite as much as if you had it at $50 a cyrd. The tactic on this is that the company already knows what their payout is and they don't have to look at a fluctuating payout. This would work best for covering a county. Because you don't have the high expense of travel, or staying overnight somewhere. It's up to you how you do your bids and contracts. Most companies will have your standard that you have to go by. Something else you can do is when you set up bids you can send it in as I have below. Where you show the cost and totals by the price chart and then post the bundle bid. That way the asset company can see the savings. And then hopefully you'll be more likely to get awarded the bid.

One thing you have to watch for is that the companies that you work for need to get their cut as well. So you need to know that if you do a bundle at $750 if they are taking their 20% out of that $750, or if they're going to add 20% to that to get their cut. If they're taking 20%, you'll pocket $600, and your budget for materials at $100 and total profit at $500. $500 is fair pay for a day worth of work. But if you employ a crew to do all the work, then you might have to add 20%. Put the bundle price at $900, the asset company takes their cut, then you take your 20% cut, and the rest goes to the crew. So that ends up being 20% to the asset company, 20% to you, and 60% payout at $540 and your profit is at $180. But I've also hired people at $100 a day for debris removal, or $8 an hour for a general laborer. These are just what I do, you'll need to figure out what works best for you, so you are still making money and able to maintain and increase your business.

Bundle

Winterize (dry Heat)	$ 125
Maid service	$ 155
Debris removal (up to 20 cyrds) $20 per cyrd over 20 cyrds	$435 up to 35 cyrds . add $20 per cubic yard over 20 cyrds. Get approval bid if over 40 cyrds.
Secure (1 lock)	$60
Lockbox	$20
Initial yard maintenance	$125

Bundle Price $750

Taking Pictures

When taking pictures there will be little differences in the pictures that need to be taken, depending on what company or companies you are working for. For a standard drive-by inspection(property verification), you'll just take one picture of the front of the house, close-up pictures of the address, and a picture showing down the street. The standard exterior pictures for preservation work is shown below:

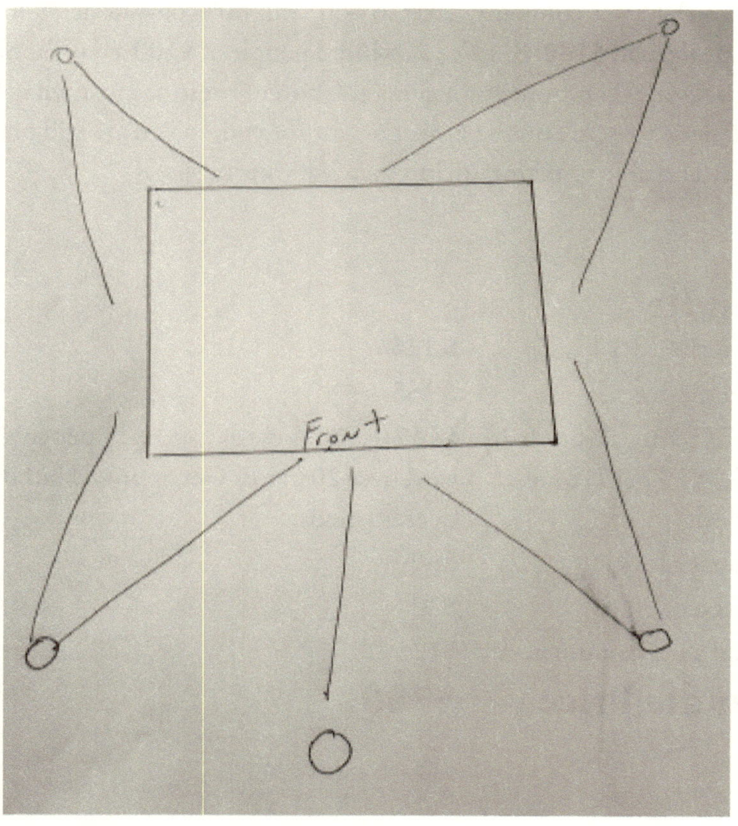

Diagram showing where to stand when taking pictures of the house and yard.

When taking pictures you take pictures from 4 corners. You start with a picture standing directly in front of the property, then go to the far corners of the property. You should be far enough to be able to get the full front of the house and a little bit of the side and also get a fair amount of the yard. And then at that same corner, you'll be able to take another picture and get mostly the side and a little bit of the front. When you do yard maintenance you'll want to do the before and after cut pictures at the same angles.

Interior Picture Requirements:

When taking pictures of the interior, you would normally take two pictures of each room trying to get the ceiling and flooring in the pictures. Sometimes the rooms are too small and you'll need to take a corner shot, then a picture of the floor and one of the ceiling. Then you would take pictures of anything that would need to be done as far as getting a house to compliance. If there is debris, or personal items, broken window, wires that need a wire nut, missing covers for light switches or receptacles, mold damage, leaking ceiling. Pictures of damages, like stains on the wall or floor and holes in the wall. When taking pictures of damages, take a distance and up-close pictures. You would also need pictures of the furnace or heater, water heater, water meter, attic, and crawl space.

To take a more thorough set of pictures, you would take pictures standing in each corner of the room, then take a picture straight up at the ceiling, and then take a picture straight down at the floor.

When taking pictures it is good practice to take double pictures of the street sign, address, window tags, sign-in sheets, winterization tag (up close so you can see the date),

Exterior Picture Requirements:

Front of the house, down the street, side of the house, back of the house, distance and close-up picture of window tag, address, street sign, lockbox, electric meter, gas meter, exterior ac unit, roof. Some companies require up-close pictures of the roof and chimney.

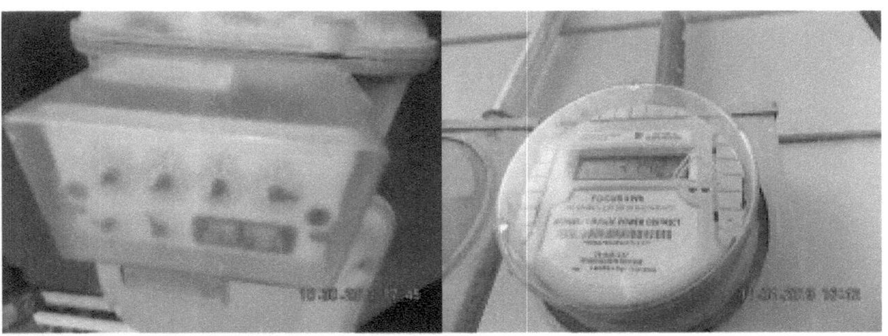

Chapter 2
Forms

Most companies will have their own forms. Some will ask you for a copy of yours. If you are going to contract directly with the mortgage companies, banks, brokers, realtor companies, then you will have your own forms already set and ready to go. When I'm out running around working on work orders I take my standard files, several copies of the forms below. It's always good to have 10 to 20 copies of the forms (maid service, winterization, property verification, grass cut, the winterization tags, lockout notification). That way if you are out on the road and get a call on work, you have some standard tags that should work for the work order.

Work order
Number

Property Verification Form

Contracting Company: _______________________________

Loan Number: _______________________________

Mortgagor: _______________________________

Address: _______________________________

Occupancy:

    ◯Mortgagor ◯ Vacant
◯Tenant ◯ Partial Vacant
◯Unknown

Color:
◯White ◯ Yellow ◯ Brown ◯ Beige/tan
◯Grey ◯ Green ◯ Blue
◯ Pink
◯Other:

____

Siding Type:
◯Wood ◯ Tin ◯ Vinyl
◯ Asbestos
◯Stucco ◯ Brick/block/ stone
◯Other

____

Roof:
◯Asphalt ◯ Wood
◯Tile ◯ Tin ◯ Aluminum
Broken Windows:

____

Boarded Windows:

____

Grass Height: _______________
Comments:

Property Value: _______________
For Sale: Y / N LockBox: Y / N
Realty Name:

____

Realty Number:

____

Type Of Property:
◯Single Family ◯ Manufactured Home
◯Duplex ◯ Commercial
◯Triplex ◯ Mobil Home
◯Fourplex ◯ Vacant Land
◯Condo ◯ Other:

____

Stories: _________
Garage:
◯attached ◯ Detached ◯ Carport
◯Shed ◯ Quonset ◯ Barn
Utilities:
Electric: ◯ On ◯ Off ◯ Unknown
Water: ◯ On ◯ Off ◯ Unknown
Gas: ◯ On ◯ Off ◯ Unknown
Personal Property:

Required pics: take double pics: front of the house, address, down the street, corner sign

Example pics:

If the property is found vacant. You would want to confirm with the neighbor. Then when it's confirmed, you would want to take pictures of all 4 sides of the house, the electric meter, and the gas meter. Some companies may want you to call it in and make your

report, especially during wintertime and there would be a need to get a winterization done as quickly as possible.

Work Order #:________________________________

Date Due: __________________________________

Business:

____

Contact Number:

____

Email:

____

Website:

____

Yard Maitenance

Client: ____

Mortgagor: ___________________________________

Address: _____________________________________

Lot Size: _______ X _________   ⬭Initial Cut: $ ______

Square Feet: ____________   ⬭Re-Cut: $ ______

⬭edge

⬭Trim trees and brush

Total: ________ Size: _________   **Any New Damages:**

⬭Debris removal cyrd: _____________

⬭Interior inspection

Recurring mow Dates:

Standard Mow Pics: Front of the house, down the sidewalk, sides of the house, the back yard, ruler measuring the grass, two pics of mowing the front, 2 pics mowing the back, at least 2 pics of weed eating and/or edging. Make sure to get weed eating the sidewalk and driveway. The after photos (pictures after the work is done) of the front of the house, down the sidewalk, sides of the house and back yard, measuring the grass showing under 2 inches, address, street sign, window tag.

If trimming bushes: would need to show before pics, measurement in linear feet, show several during pictures of work being done, and after pics. Full exterior pics before and full exterior pics after. Show debris, Picture of trailer empty, show measurement of the trailer, pics of debris in the trailer, pics of place cards. A place card can be written out on a little whiteboard, or piece of paper.

Place card example:

```
Trailer 7x16    load 1

    3 cyrds

    tree limbs
```

Example pics:

When taking pics, you should do your before and after pics at the same angles to the property. You'll do your before pics, pics of mowing, pics of weed eating, and then your set of after pics. Sometimes it's good to have a pic of your vehicle there. I'd suggest having business magnets on your vehicle to identify your business. It's good for advertisement, plus it also identifies you as a specialist working there. If you have to rake leaves, then bag them, and take pictures of all the bags before throwing them away. Or at least have the leaves up in a pile showing the pile there, then after your remove the pile, show it gone. The main pictures you would need for an initial mow, are all four sides of the house, showing the house and quite a bit of the yard, picture of the address and/or corner sign, picture of mowing, edging, and after pics. During the initial mow or first mow, you would also trim the shrubs. Make sure no shrubs or trees are touching the house. They should be 12 inches away from the house. And below the windows. Sometimes trimming shrubs is part of the initial work order, sometimes trimming shrubs is an extra charge that you can bill out or bid. Sometimes you will need to bid leaf removal. There be yard waste removal fees that you can charge. Some companies expect you to remove them as part of the standard yard service.

Snow Removal: for snow removal, most companies will require at least 3 inches of snow on the ground in order for you to be paid. You would take pictures of all 4 sides of the house, then down the sidewalk, and driveway. Take a few during pictures, vehicle pictures, then after pictures. Then you would have to salt the stairs and walkways. Then the rest of the standard exterior pics (electric meter, gas meter, address, street sign, distance, and up-close picture of the window tag)

Recut List

City Address Lockbox Code Key code Due Date

Initial Inspection

On this form, you may get an order to do an interior/exterior inspection or initial secure and you either fix items that have an approved allowable or bid everything that needs to be fixed to get the house into compliance. This would depend on what the work order asks for and whether or not it's presale or post-sale. Some of the top things to look at are if the property is secure (check the doors and make sure they are able to lock, check windows, if the windows need a lock or to be boarded), debris, personal items, infestation risks. You may get an order just to do the inspection, or you may get an order to do an "initial" which could consist of a lock change, secure all outbuildings and garages. Which would mean that you would put a padlock and hasp on the outbuilding door, garage door pedestrian door, and in the railing of the overhead door. Then depending on what time of year it is you may be approved to do a winterization on the property and/or a yard initial mow. Yard initial mows would include mow, edging the sidewalks and driveway, weed-eating along the fence line and around the house, trimming trees or brush so no tree or brush is touching the house (must be 12 inches away from the house). Some work orders may have that as part of an initial, then do an inspection and place a bid on debris removal or whatever else that needs to be done to bring it up to code. Some work orders may want you to do a full initial and clean out. Which would be lawn service, winterization (if in season), debris removal, maid service, boarding if needed (then bid to reglaze). Some may also have an allowable for roof repair and pest control. You'll just need to make sure you read everything on the work order.

The initial inspection is something you need to be very thorough on. You need good pictures and good documentation. This helps to prove your job was done correctly and may also help get approval for more work.

Standard pictures for initial inspection:

Exterior pictures:

Front of house, side of the house, back of the house, address, street sign, AC unit, roof (you'll have to get on the roof and take several pictures), electric meter, gas meter, pictures of debris, and place card with total cubic yards, measure grass height, trees or bushes that need to be trimmed with length measurements, window tag at a distance and up close (close enough to read the phone number), Lock box, show lock box code, lock box showing keys, keys in Knoblock, key code. If there is roof damage or a leaking ceiling you may be required to measure the damaged area. Some companies may want you to do a chalk outline of the damaged roof and ceiling areas. If you measure to repair the damaged areas, my suggestion would be to get your measurement for the bid to repair, then get a measurement of the entire roof. Some companies might allow the repair, but some might want the entire roof replaced. Some companies may have an allowable, enough to get the repair done. Then after the work is done, take your after pictures, then get a full measurement set of pictures just in case at a later time a work order is passed to do the entire roof.

Interior pictures:

sign-in sheet, each room pictures standing in every 4 corners of the room, Ceiling, and floor, inside toilets, breaker box, breaker box showing breakers, water meter, water heater, and furnace. In each room that had debris, you'll have to make a place card and take a picture of the place card (place card can be done on a whiteboard or scratch paper). Take pictures of underneath the sinks, pictures of cabinets with doors closed and doors open. Take a picture of winterization tags showing the date of winterization.

Place card example:

Bedroom 1

5 cyrd of debris

living room

10 cyrds of debris

This is done for each room and you write out any discrepancies.

Work order
Number

Initial Inspection Form

Vendor Code _____________________ **Completion Date:** _____________

Company Name_______________________________________

Conttractor's Name: _________________________________

Contractor's Address: _______________________________

Fax#: ___________________________________

E-mail: ____   Website:

____

Ph#: ___________________________________

Client: _______________________________ **Client Phone Number:**

____

Loan Number_________________________

Work order Number_________________

Property Address_______________________________________

Occupancy Status: Occupied _______ Vacant _____ Partial ___

Occupied

by:____

How

Verified:____

If   partial,   which   units   were

vacant?____

Violation Posted: ____

Mobil   Home:_____Mobile   Home   Park   Name:

____

Mobile Home Park Number: ___________________________

Hud Number: ______________________________   serial Number:

____

Property Description:

Is the Property For Sale? Y N Contact Info:

Name   of
Realtor____
    Phone Number_________________________ Active Listing? Y N
    Violations/Citations   Posted?   Y   N   If   yes,   for
what?_______________________

Securing

Secure upon arrival? Y N If no, why?____

Secure upon departure Y N

Locks

Lock Change completed? Y N Key Code___________

Location/Quantities: Front______ Rear______ Secondary______ Garage_______

Locked by Others? Y N Key Code___________ Location(s)__________

Lock box installed? Y N Lock box code______

Padlock Installed? Y N

Location/Quantities: Front___ Rear___ Secondary___ Garage___ Outbuilding___

Pool Gate___

Number of Slide Bolts Installed: ________

Location(s)____

Number of Slider Locks Installed: _______

Location(s)____

Number of window Locks installed: ___

Locations:

Boarding

Is Boarding Needed: Y N

Qty _______ Size: _________

____

____

____

Was Boarding Completed: Y N
If No, why: ____

Window(s)

Qty ________Location:________________Size: Length _____ Width
_____

Qty_________ Location______________ Size:
Length_______Width___________

Door(s)

Qty _______Location ______________ Size: Length_______ Width
____

Qty_________ Location_________________ Size: Length_______ x
Width___________

Winterization

Completed?   Y   N   If   no,
why?____

Dry___ Dry/Well___ Steam_____ Steam/Well_____ Radiant _____
Radiant/Well___

Is there a Sump Pump? Y N If so, is it operable? Y N
Is   Water   Off   at   the   Curb?   Y   N   If   no,
why?___________________________________

Common Utilities? Y N
Bid to Thaw (if required) $___________

Method   of   Thawing   (type   of
heaters)____

Number of Men Required to Thaw___________ Hours Needed to
Thaw___________

Damages

Mortgagor Neglect Y N

Eyeball Estimate $_____________

Detailed   Description
(required)____

____

Vandalism Y N

Eyeball Estimate $___________

____

____

Freeze Damage Y N

Eyeball Estimate $_____________

Detailed   Description
(required)____

____

Water Damage Y N

Eyeball Estimate $__________

Area Size _________Location_____________________ Possible
Cause____

Detailed   Description
(required)____

____

Fire Damage Y N

Eyeball Estimate $________________

Detailed   Description
(required)____

Storm Damage Y N Eyeball Estimate $__________

Detailed   Description
(required)____

Unfinished Renovation Y N Eyeball Estimate $______________

Detailed   Description
(required)____

____

Structural Damage Y N Eyeball Estimate $______________

Detailed   Description
(required)____

____

Environmental Damage Y N Eyeball Estimate $______________

Detailed   Description
(required)____

____

Mold Damage Y N Eyeball Estimate $______________

Area Size: ______________ Location_____________________________

Possible Cause_____ __________________

Detailed   Description
(required)____

____

Bid to Clean/Treat Mold $______ Bid to Remove Mold
$______________

Roof Damage Y N Eyeball Estimate $______________

Area Size______________ Location______________________________

Possible   Cause______________________________________

____

Detailed   Description

(required)____ __________

____

Active Leak Y N Flat __________ Pitch ______________

Type: Asphalt   Slate   Shingle   Tin   Other

____

Bid to Tarp $______ Bid to Patch $______ Bid to Replace

$________

Grass Cuts

Grass

Initial Grass Cut Completed? Y N If no, why? (Circle one)

Limited Growth - Debris in the way - Not for the allowable - No grass - Realtor Maintaining - Condo Association Maintaining - Cut by Others - Out of Season Other: ______________

Lot   Size: Length______   x   Width______   Height__

____

Shrubs

Shrubs Trimmed? Y N If not, why?______________________________

Linear Feet __________________ Qty____________

Debris

Exterior Debris

CYDS________ Potential Violation? Y N In way of Grass Cut? Y

N

Description____

Removed? Y N If no, Bid to Remove $__________

Interior Health Hazards

CYDS________

Description____

Removed? Y N If no, Bid to Remove $__________

Garage Debris

CYDS: _______________

Description:

____

____

Removed? Y N If no, Bid to Remove: $______________

Personals

CYDS______

Description____

Estimated Value $___________

Bid to Remove $____________ Bid to Store $__________

Health Hazards

Paint Gal / Can (circle one) Qty ___________ Bid $____________

Chemicals/Cleaners Gal / Can (circle one) Qty __________ Bid
$___________

Oil Gal / Can (circle one) Qty ___________ Bid $___________

Paint Thinner Gal / Can (circle one) Qty __________ Bid
$___________

Gas Can/s Gal / Can (circle one) Qty __________ Bid
$___________

Tires Qty___________ Bid $___________

Batteries Qty___________ Bid $____________

Propane Tank Qty____________ Bid $___________

Vehicles Qty: _____

Make: _________Model: ________________ Serial   Number:
____

Make: _________Model: ________________ Serial   Number:
____

Make: _________Model: ________________ Serial   Number:
____

Miscellaneous Bids

Extermination Needed? Y N

Property Infested with: (circle all that apply)

Mice   Rats   Roaches   Ants   Bees   Termites   Fleas
Other___________________________

Bid to Exterminate $________________

Bid provided by a Professional Exterminator? Y N (required)

Name of Exterminator: ___________________

Phone Number of Exterminator: ______________________________

Basement Flooded? Y N

Bid to Pump the Basement $_________

Height of water ____________

Possible
Cause____

Other Bids

    1. Description:____

       Bid $__________

    2. Description:____

       Bid $__________

    3. Description:____

Bid $__________

4. Description:____

    Bid $__________

5. Description:____

    Bid $__________

Standard Land Fill Reciept/Form

LandFill Name:
Address:

0000

Cash Customer   **PO#: 0101**

Date In _________

Time In _________

Date Out _______

Time Out ________

Gross Weight

Tare Weight 7000

Net Weight

Cost Per Ton: $40

Total $00.00

State Tax   00

County Tax   00

Net Cash Amount $00.00

LandFill Name:

Address:

Phone:

Debris removal pics requirements:

First, you'll do a full initial interior/exterior set of pictures and then a place card for exterior, and place card for each room in the house that has debris.

Example of Place cards:

```
     Bedroom 1                living room


  5 cyrd of debris         10 cyrds of debris




  exterior debris


     15 cyrds
```

Take a picture of the empty trailer, measurement of the trailer (width and length), pictures of place cards when the trailer is ¼, ½,3/4, and full.

```
Trailer 7 x 16 load 1
                         Trailer 7 x 16 load 1
       1/4 full
                                1/2 full
```

```
Trailer 7 x 16 load 1


       3/4 load
```

```
Trailer 7 x 16 load 1

        Full

    17 cyrds
```

Good documentation helps assure that you get paid for everything you do.

Work order
Number

Work Completion Form

Vendor Code _______________ **Completion Date:** __________

Company Name________________________________

Contractor's Name: __________________________

Contractor's Address: ________________________

Tax ID#: _______________

Ph#: __________________________

Fax#: _________________________

E-mail__________________________

Client: __________________________ **Client Phone Number:** ________________

Loan Number_____________________

Work order Number________________

Property Address___________________________________

1.   Work   Completed   ________________________________ $__________

2. Work Completed _______________________________ $__________

3.   Work Completed_______________________________ $__________

4.   Work Completed_______________________________ $__________

5.   Work   Completed   ________________________________ $__________

6. Work Completed _______________________________ $__________

7.   Work Completed____

$___________

8.   Work Completed____

$___________

9.   Work Completed____

$___________

Total $___________

Comments:

A sign in sheet will need to be placed on a kitchen counter or taped to the wall by the main entrance door.

Sign in Sheet

Company Name: ________________________

Contact Address: ____________________________

Contact Phone Number: ____________________________

ADDRESS:

Date Name Company Reason

____

Business

____

Contact number

Maid Service Check Off List

(initial each when completed)

______ Clean refrigerator

______ broom sweep all carpets and floors

______ Mop floors

______ Clean Toilets

______ Wipe down kitchen sinks, countertops, and cabinets

______ wipe down the bathroom sink, countertops, and cabinets

_______ Wipe down windows, window trim, and baseboards
_______ brush off any cobwebs
_______ Wipe off all out-let and light switch covers
_______ Wipe off light covers and ceiling fan blades
_______ Place an air freshener in the bathrooms and kitchen and add a date and initials in marker on the air freshener
_______ Broom sweep garage and brush off cobwebs
_______ General walk around and check for Conveyance
Maid Refresh Dates

Maid service standards:

You'll start off with an initial set of interior and exterior pictures. Then you would take pictures of work being done called "during pictures." I usually start with the top and work my way down. I usually start with a duster and dust window seals, shelves, sinks, countertops, dusting of ceiling fans, dust on top of doors, dust on the door trim, dust on the base boards. After I do a quick dusting I go into wipe down mode. I start with the kitchen. Wipe down the sink, countertop, inside and outside the cabinets. cleaning toilets, cleaning refrigerators and stove and ovens, sweeping the floor, moping the floor, picture of air freshener with dates on them (you would need to put an air freshener in the kitchen and each bathroom and utility room), picture of wiping off light switch covers, and a picture of the maid sign off sheet, sign-in sheet. And identify any safety hazards, leaks, or mold. Most companies will want you to pull out any nails or screws that are in the walls. Then do another full set of pictures for your after shots. So you end up with before, during, and after photos.

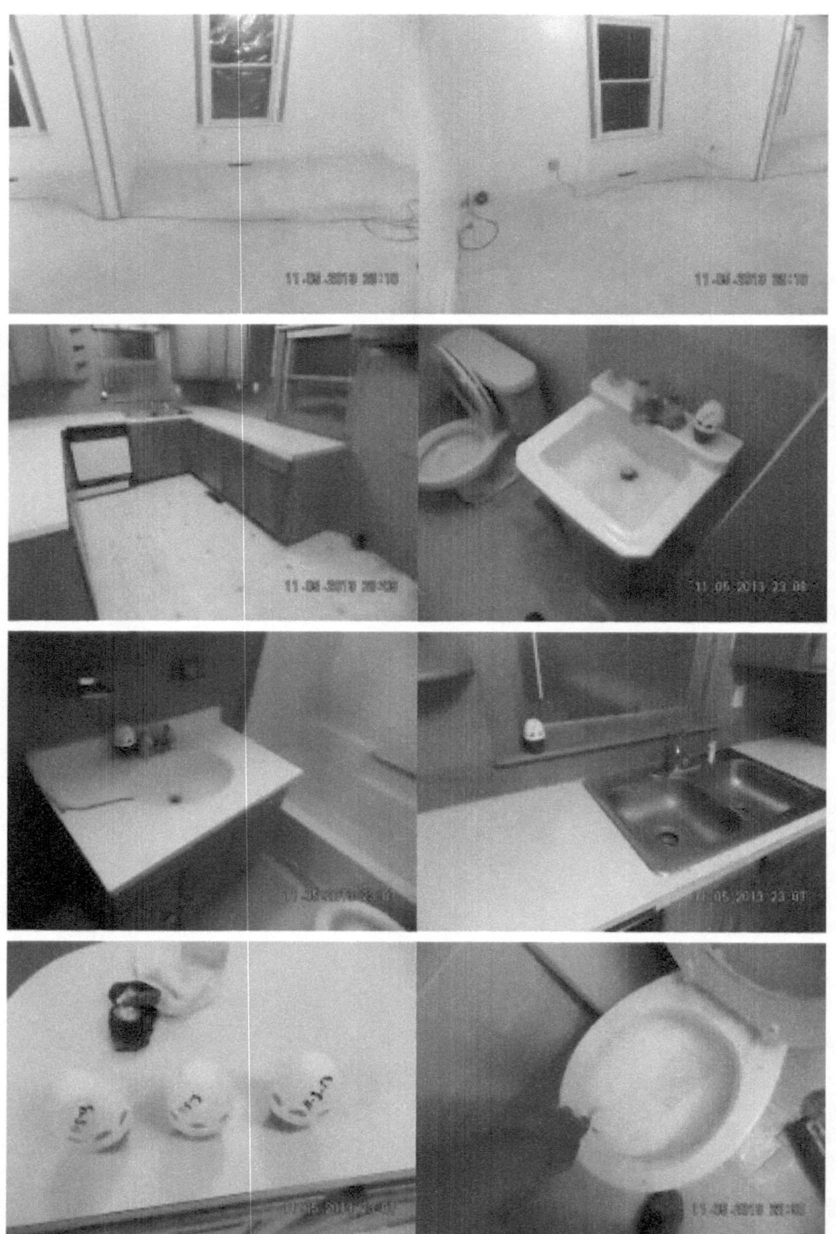

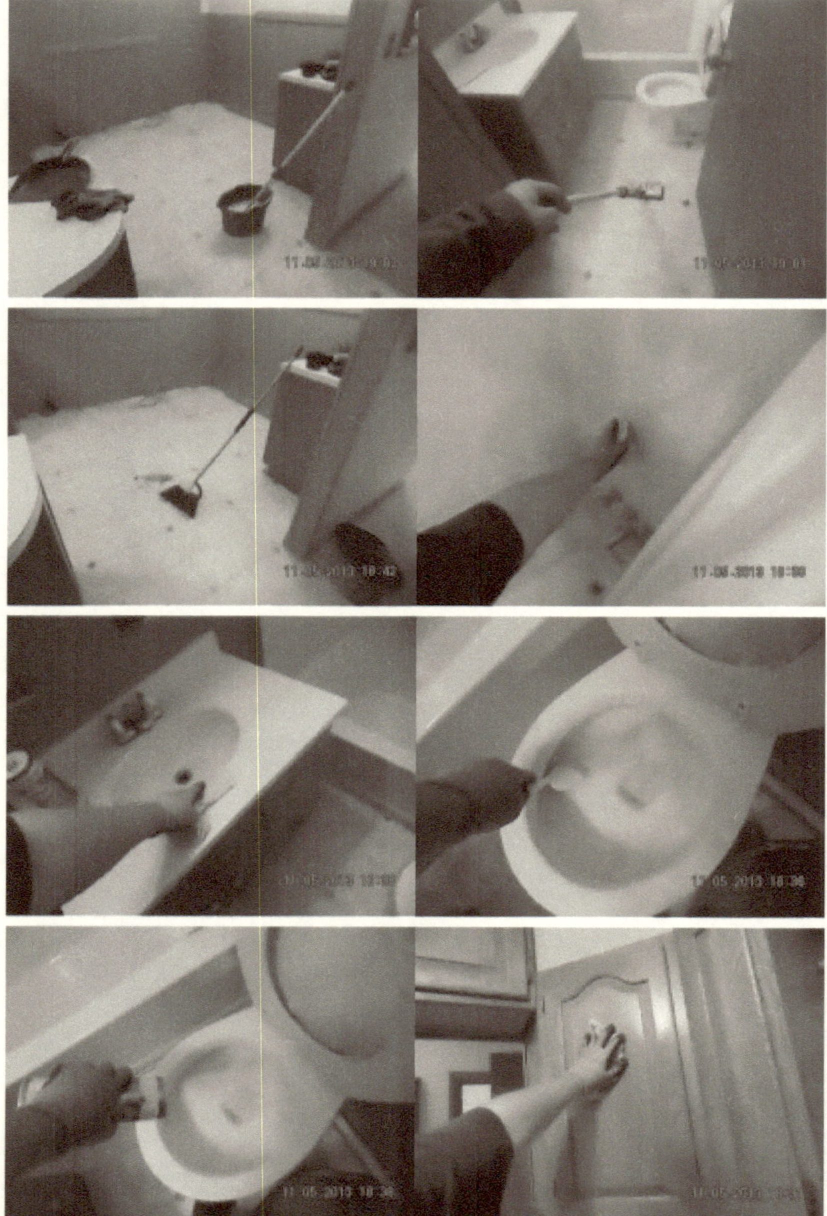

Pictures for maid refresh:

Maid refreshes should only take about 10 or 15 minutes to do. You'll need to take your standard exterior pictures, pictures of the electric meter, gas meter, water meter, water heater, heating unit, at least one picture of every room, inside the toilet, sign-in sheet, and dusting. You'll need to make sure you get a picture of dusting the kitchen cabinets, window, sink, bathroom sink, toilet, tub, ceiling fan, molding, door, door trim. If the floor gets dirty because of people walking through, then there may be a need to mop or vacuum (some work orders require it, some don't)

130

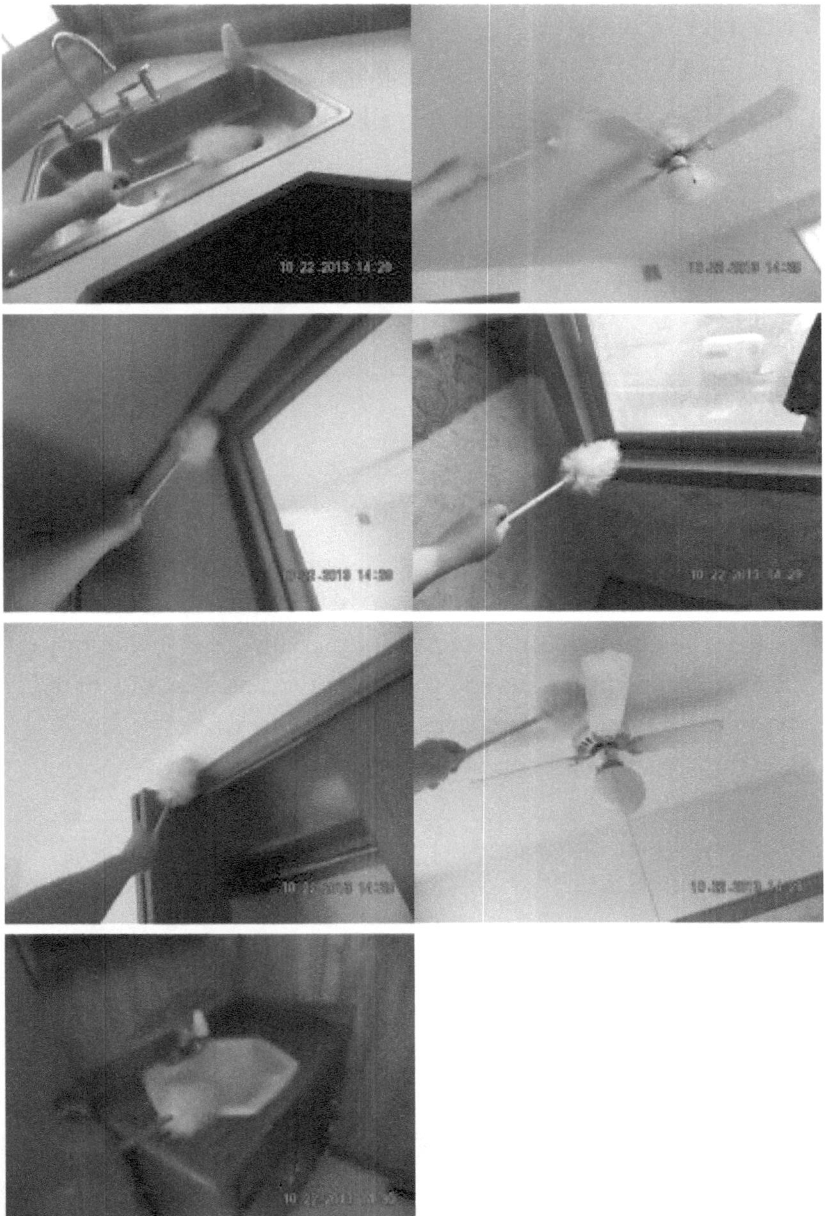

BUSINESS NAME: ______________________________

14 DAY NOTICE OF RIGHT TO RECLAIM ABANDONED PERSONAL PROPERTY

Date:

To:

____

(name of former Occupant)

Address:

____

(Address of former Occupant)

When you vacated the premises at:

____

(address of premises)

Some personal property remained (see personal property list)

Unless you notify us no later than 14 days after the date of this notice that the personal property has not been abandoned and of your intent to claim it, and unless you pay the reasonable cost of storage, if any, we will dispose of this property in accordance with state law.

You may claim this property at

____

(Address where property may be claimed)

BUSINESS NAME: ______________________________

PERSONAL PROPERTY INVENTORY LIST

Date:

Property Address

Personal Property Description Quantity

Winterization Check List

Work Order #: _______________________
    Address:

____

_____ Shut off water at the curb
_____ Turn off main in the house
_____ zip tie the shut-off valve
_____ disconnect the water meter and blow out the meter
_____ cap the feed line
_____ drain the water heater
_____ blow out the water lines
_____ pressure test the lines to 30 lbs for 30 seconds
_____ make sure toilettes are clean
_____ pour RV antifreeze in each drain (kitchen sink, bathroom sink, tub, shower toilette)
_____ install plastic wrap over the toilette
_____ install winterization stickers
_____ if no sump pump, turn off breaker and tag
_____ visual check of system for compliance
Note:

Winterization standard pics for dry winterization:

You'll start off with a full set of interior and exterior pics, then you'll need a picture of the water heater, a hose connected to the water heater, show water draining out of the hose, water meter before disconnect, water meter after connect, the main valve before shut off, the main water valve after shutoff, main water valve with a zip tie, show utilities on and off by taking pictures of light off, then light on, picture of your generator or inverter, up-close picture of a generator showing watts. electrical box with the breaker on, then breaker box with the main breaker in off position, air compressor, pressure gage reading 30 lbs, showing air compressor (some companies want a minimum 8-gallon compressor) and air hose hooked up to water line and blowing out lines and pressure gage at 30 lbs, Picture of a watch showing start and ending time of pressure test. The pressure test should last 30 minutes. show water coming out of each faucet. Need pictures of winterization tags on each sink, toilet, tub, shower, water heater, water meter, washer valves, front door, or window. Show pouring RV antifreeze down each drain (sink, shower, tub, toilet, toilet tank, floor drain, washer drain), wrap on the toilet, and picture of winterization sign-off sheet. If there is a sump pump, you would need to take a picture of that, and a picture of you testing the pump to make sure it is working correctly. And if there is a sump pump, then the utilities need to be turned on if not on already. The contracting company may have a company name and address to put the utilities under or you may need to contact them to have them set it up.

Broken Line: In case you pressure test, and the test fails because of broken water lines. You would take some masking tape and put it on the broken line near the break. Write a number on the tape and take a picture. You do that for each break. And then measure the length of the waterline you'll need to replace and take a picture of the tape measurement. Take a distance picture and an up-close picture to give a good overall view of the breaks.

Note: If in your winterization, you have to disconnect the water meter and plug the main feed line, you would want to check your local ordinance to make sure that you are allowed to do that. In some areas, only the city is allowed to do that, or a licensed plumber.

Note II: When using a generator, several companies want pictures of the generator, and some companies what you to back feed. Back feeding is when you have an extension cord with 2 male plug ends so you can plug your generator into an outlet. This is something that can be very dangerous to do. And In some areas, may be illegal. Check with your city and state ordinances before attempting this. If there is bad wiring in the house, it could cause a fire. You would want to double-check and make sure the main breaker is off. If a breaker is left on, and the city is working on a wiring issue, and your back feeding a house, could electrocute that person that could be working on the mainline. But breakers can fail. So even turning off the main breaker, breakers can fail so there is always a chance that you could back feed through the main feed. You want to check with the city and state ordinance as well as an electrician. Most companies have stopped requiring back feeding.

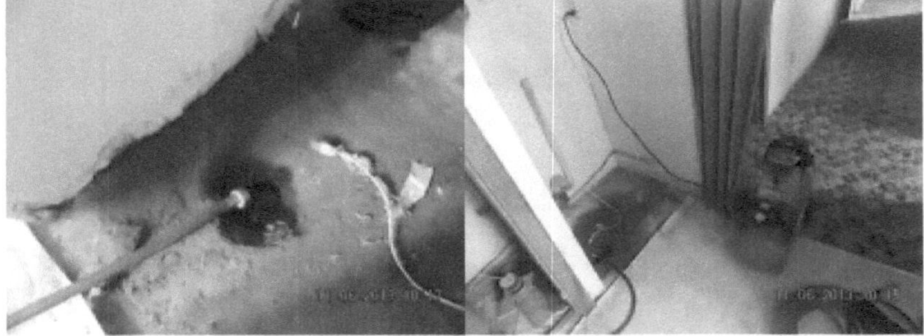

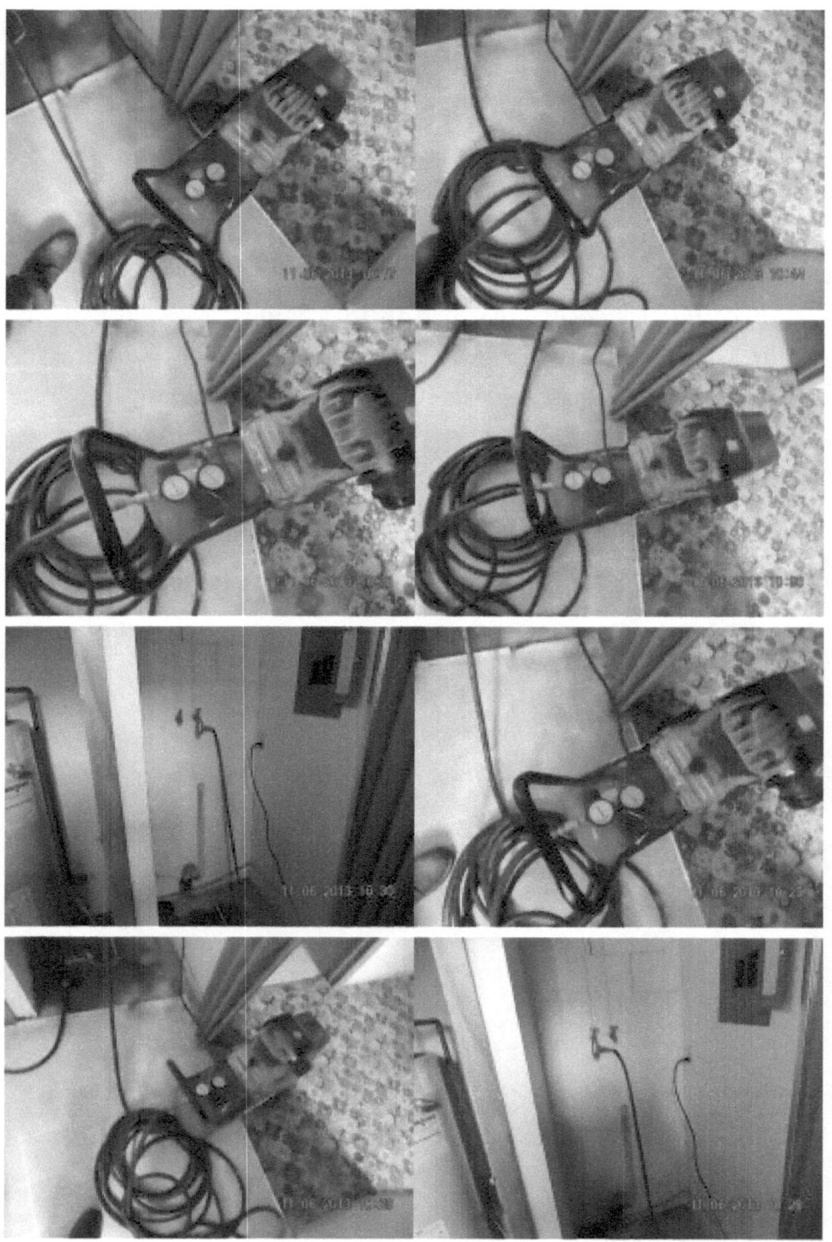

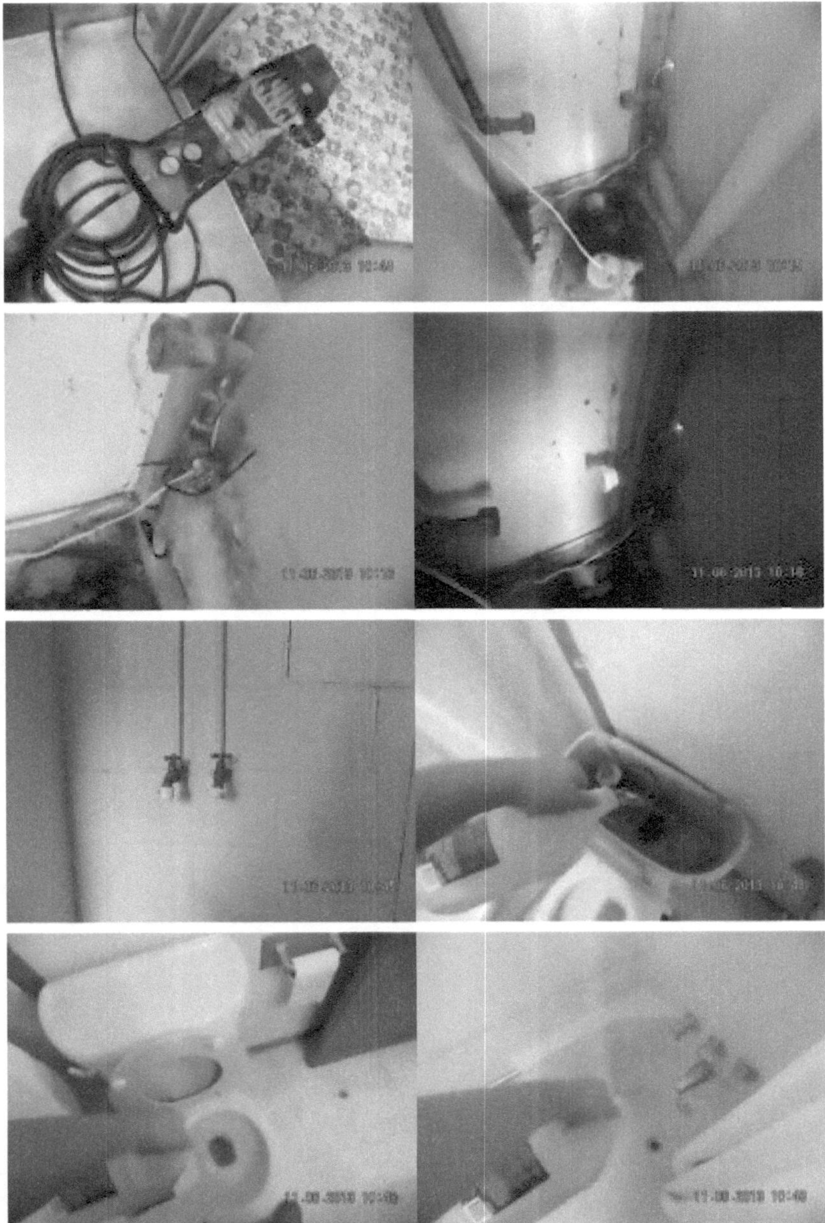

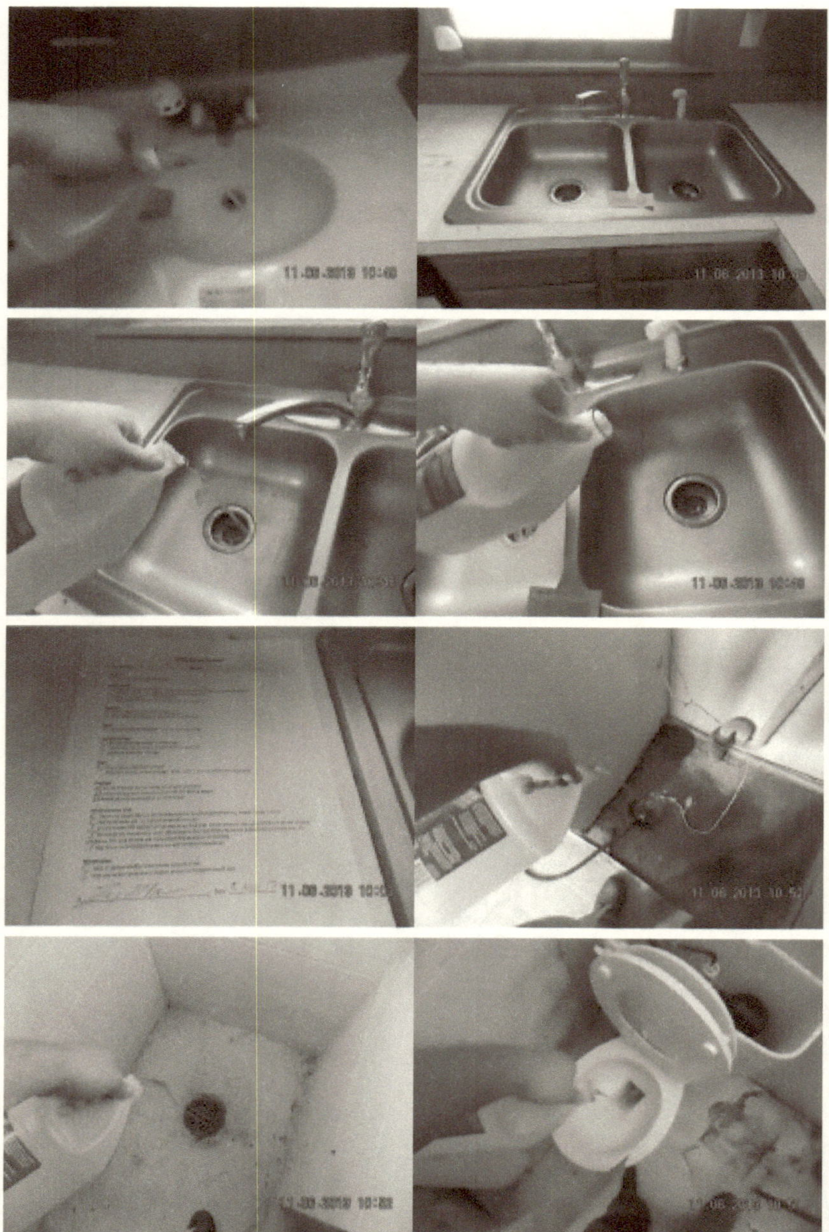

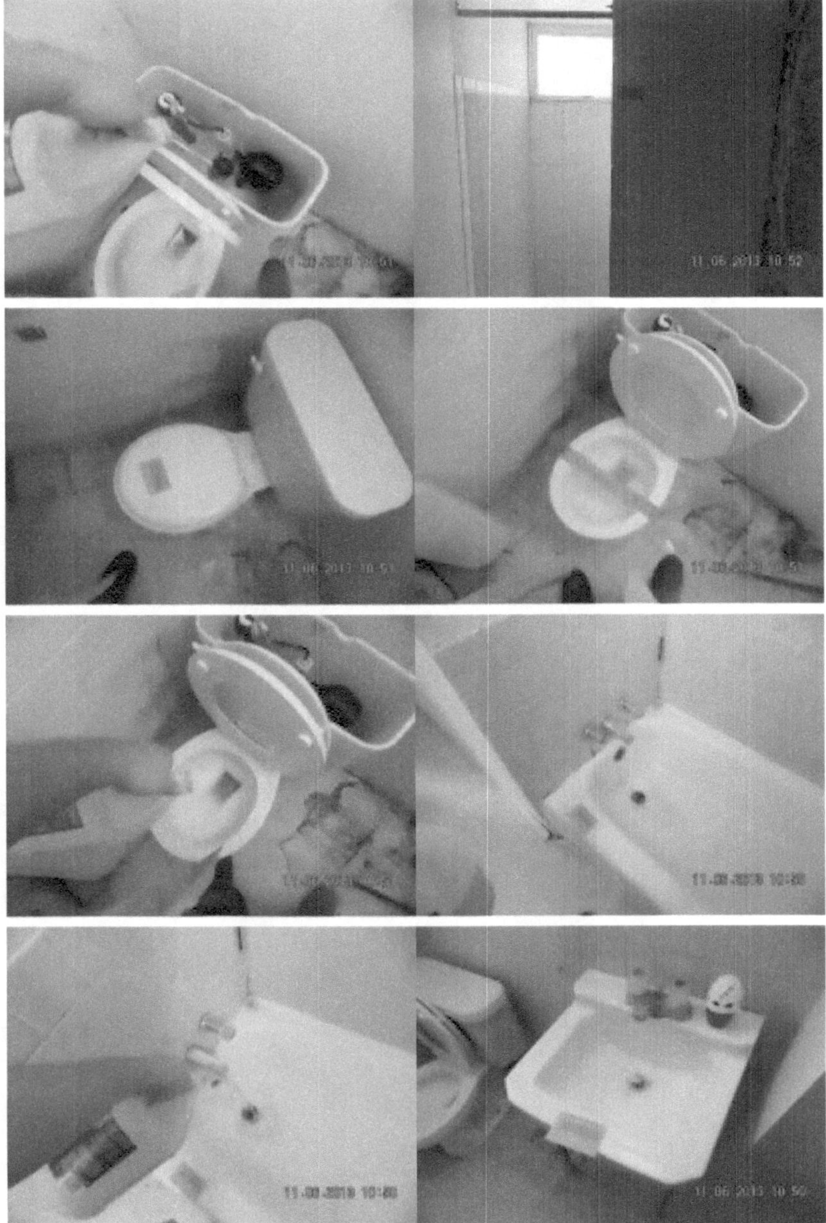

Below is a standard adaptor that you can use to put on a valve for a washer. ¾ x ¾ x ½ T, with a plug on one end, and a nipple and cap on the other end on the ½ there is a ½ to 3/8 reducer and a connector for an air compressor. On the second adapter, I added a washer hose. I had to put a couple of washers on it so that it sealed well, but the second adapter has been more useful and can get into areas that the other can't.

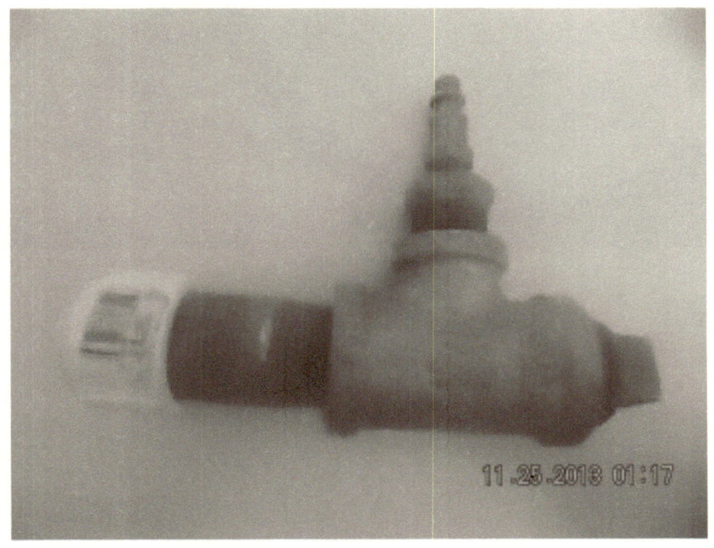

Winterized

Date: ____/____/____

Company: ___________________________

<u>A winterization has been performed at this property pursuant to a work order issued by your mortgage company.</u>

Work completed: water meter disconnected, zip tie on shut off valve, water heater drained, line has blown out with forced air, RV anti-freeze pored in each drain and the toilette. Please be advised to have a licensed plumber inspect all lines for any leaking when reconnecting.

Winterized

Date: ___ / ___ / ___

Company: ________________________

<u>A winterization has been performed at this property pursuant to a work order issued by your mortgage company.</u>

Work completed: water meter disconnected, zip tie on shut off valve, water heater drained, line blown out with forced air, RV anti-freeze pored in each drain and the toilette. Please be advised to have a licensed plumber inspect all lines for any leaking when reconnecting.

Winterized

Date: ___/___/___

Company: ____________________

A winterization has been performed at this property pursuant to a work order issued by your mortgage company.

Work completed: water meter disconnected, zip tie on shut off valve, water heater drained, line blown out with forced air, RV anti-freeze pored in each drain and the toilette. Please be advised to have a licensed plumber inspect all lines for any leaking when reconnecting.

Winterized

Date: ___/___/___

Company: ____________________

A winterization has been performed at this property pursuant to a work order issued by your mortgage company.

Work completed: water meter disconnected, zip tie on shut off valve, water heater drained, line blown out with forced air, RV anti-freeze pored in each drain and the toilette. Please be advised to have a licensed plumber inspect all lines for any leaking when reconnecting.

Winterized

Date: ___/___/___

Company: ____________________

A winterization has been performed at this property pursuant to a work order issued by your mortgage company.

Winterized

Date: ___/___/___

Company: ____________________

A winterization has been performed at this property pursuant to a work order issued by your mortgage company.

Work completed: water meter disconnected, zip tie on shut off valve, water heater drained, line blown out with forced air, RV anti-freeze pored in each drain and the toilette. Please be advised to have a licensed plumber inspect all lines for any leaking when reconnecting.

Winterized

Date: ___/___/___

Company: ____________________

A winterization has been performed at this property pursuant to a work order issued by your mortgage company.

Work completed: water meter disconnected, zip tie on shut off valve, water heater drained, line blown out with forced air, RV anti-freeze pored in each drain and the toilette. Please be advised to have a licensed plumber inspect all lines for any leaking when reconnecting.

Winterized

Date: ___/___/___

Company: ____________________

A winterization has been performed at this property pursuant to a work order issued by your mortgage company.

Work completed: water meter disconnected, zip tie on shut off valve, water heater drained, line blown out with forced air, RV anti-freeze pored in each drain and the toilette. Please be advised to have a licensed plumber inspect all lines for any leaking when reconnecting.

Winterized

Date: ___/___/___

Company: ___________________

A winterization has been performed at this property pursuant to a work order issued by your mortgage company.

Work completed: water meter disconnected, zip tie on shut off valve, water heater drained, line blown out with forced air, RV anti-freeze pored in each drain and the toilette. Please be advised to have a licensed plumber inspect all lines for any leaking when reconnecting.

Work completed: water meter disconnected, zip tie on shut off valve, water heater drained, line blown out with forced air, RV anti-freeze pored in each drain and the toilette. Please be advised to have a licensed plumber inspect all lines for any leaking when reconnecting.

Winterized

Date: ___/___/___

Company: ___________________

A winterization has been performed at this property pursuant to a work order issued by your mortgage company.

Work completed: water meter disconnected, zip tie on shut off valve, water heater drained, line blown out with forced air, RV anti-freeze pored in each drain and the toilette. Please be advised to have a licensed plumber inspect all lines for any leaking when reconnecting.

Steps for Winterization

Step 1: The first thing you would want to do, is to take a walk through the house, evaluate things, check to see if the electricity is on, and check to see if the water is on. If the water is turned off at the curb you can start prepping for the winterization. If the electricity is turned off, then shut the break-off. Take before and after pictures of the breaker being turned off, and put a winterization sticker on the breaker box. The breaker needs to be turned off for when the city turns the electricity back there is less likely to have damage done by an electric heater running with no water in it, or a stove or oven turned on. It is a safety precaution to turn the main breaker off. If you already have electricity on, then you don't have to use your generator, but after your done with the winterization you'll need to turn off the breaker and tag it.

Step 2: The next step You would do is shut off the main water feed valve on the inside of the house and put a zip tie on the valve and tag it, then disconnect the water meter and you'll need to blow the water out of the water meter. Then install a plugin on the feed line.

Step 3: Then you would hook up a hose to the water heater and start draining the water heater. Hopefully, there is a drain on the same floor that the water heater is on.

Step 4: While the water heater is draining hook up your air compressor to the washer water line and blow out the water. That can help pressure the water out of the water heater. While the water is draining, check each faucet in the house by turning them on and letting the water run out of it until you have air. Make sure to get a picture of each valve with water coming out of it.

Step 5: After all the water is out of the line, shut off all your valves and pressure test at 30 pounds for 30 minutes. Take a picture of your watch at the beginning and end of the test to show 30 minutes have passed. When you're taking the pictures, you'll need pictures of the water heater, the water heater being drained, a picture of water coming out of the hose, pictures of both ends of the hose, a picture of the air compressor, several pictures of the air compressor gauges showing that it's holding at 30 lbs, pictures of the generator, picture of a light on and light off to show that electricity is hooked up and working, picture of water meter connected and disconnected, pictures of tools.

Step 6: You'll need to make sure the toilettes are cleaned, take before during, and after pictures of the cleaning. I would do this while the water heater is being drained so you have water to use. I usually bring a 5-gallon jug just in case.

Step 7: After that is done, then you are ready to pour the antifreeze down all the drains (sinks, showers, bathtubs, floor drain, toilette bowl, dishwasher, cloth washer drain, and back of toilette).

Step 8: Then put a wrap on the toilet bowl (this could be a regular plastic winterization sheet that you can order, or you can use saran wrap or plastic drop cloth. If you use a plastic drop cloth or saran wrap you would put that over the bowl, then put a piece of tape on that and write on the tape, marking it as "Winterized", "Do Not Use". After that, you would put the small winterization tag on all the sinks, toilets, tubs, water meter, water heater, front door, and you'll take a picture of that, put a winterization sticker by the kitchen sink, along with a winterization check-off list and take pictures of that. That completes the winterization.

Do a visual inspection of water lines and note any defects.

If a winterization fails place a bid on any defects. If there are breaks in the line, mark each break with a piece of masking tape. Put a number on each break. Make sure to mark it as a failed pressure test and a reason why on the winterization check-off sheet.

Tips and Tricks

Working in both fields can create a significant amount of cash flow. But if lack general maintenance skills you might consider looking for someone that does possess those skills and maybe subcontract them out.

Some companies do require that you have general liability insurance and some require you have liability insurance and EoM insurance. Not all require this, but some do and it's a good idea to have insurance. To get started you would have to create a resume. I have an example of a resume in this book on page 16. Then you would go to the websites of the companies I have listed and email your resume to them. Most will send you a package to fill out and you'll be put on their vendor list. You could get work right away. You will get emailed your assignments, some companies might call ya on a phone and email the work orders to you.

The way some companies work, they will require you to send in your pictures on their website and fill out an online form. Some companies will want you to scan and email the forms and pictures and some will want you to fax the form and email the pictures. Downloading a program like canscan allows you to scan a picture with your phone and automatically put it into PDF form. It also allows you to crop the photo.

After you get some experience under your belt, there may be a time to try and get some direct business. Rather than doing business through a contracting business, you get rid of the middle man and contract directly with the mortgage company, realtor, or broker. When you're dealing with a middleman, they'll take between 20% to 60% of the income. But they do create the business for you. Just learn from them. The different companies will have some good and some bad practices. The best thing is to learn what you think are the good practices and incorporate them into your personal business. When you expand into your own contracting company and have to hire extra help because the workload is heavy, having proper paperwork and getting it done correctly is important, but getting the workers to the jobs and completing those jobs are much more important. The reason I say that, is that I do work for some companies that if there is an error, they'll call me on the phone and confirm the error and they'll fix it for me and it doesn't waste but a minute to fix. But I have some companies that if there is the slightest error on the paperwork, they want you to redo the whole form, which could be another hour out of your time. That doesn't make you money, and it certainly doesn't make the contracting company any money. I've had companies have me reconfirm my paperwork, but to do that, I had to go back out to the property and take more pictures to reconfirm what I said. If that's 100 miles away, then that's half a day shot, and you're paying out a lot of money on gas. So it doesn't hurt to take extra pictures.

If a property is supposed to be occupied and it looks vacant, re-confirm it with a neighbor and check the electric meter and take a picture of the meter, then check and see if the water is on or off.

General tip: If you don't have a lot of money to invest into your business, then start small, with the minimum. Build up the business, test the waters and get comfortable with the inspection and/or preservation work before getting into some big expenses. That way, you work the business for a while and you know what kind of income you'll be getting in and budget for your expansion.

Yard Maintenance: when mowing a yard, you'll need to make sure to pick up the trimmings, but a way to do it real quick is just to run your mower across the sidewalk and blow the grass trimmings into the yard. If you're going to do yard service full time, then you'll want to buy a quality commercial mower.

General Inspections: when doing a drive-by inspection, you should probably dress a certain way. Being a little dressy helps. It makes it look more professional. But if you really don't want people messing with ya, wear a Kickboxing or boxing shirt and/or cap and drive up on a Harley. People will usually leave you alone.

General Info: If you are into preservation you'll need to eventually get your own power supply. The preferred way would be a generator. Probably a 5500 watt or higher. That way you can run your power tools. It'll take around a 3000-watt generator to run a fair-sized air compressor and that's probably the machine that you will use that has the highest wattage. I've used inverters that you hook up to your battery. They are a lot less expensive than a generator, but you can't run an air compressor very long on it, if at all, and a circular saw won't run on it. They'll both trip the breaker in it. Starting out, I used one, and sometimes we got lucky and was able to hook up a cord to a neighbors house. But the generator is the money maker

Rain gear: don't really need one if you just doing field inspections. But if you are doing preservation and yard maintenance they come in handy. I've had to finish up quite a few lawn care jobs in the rain. And I'd rather finish up and get a little wet than have the extra expense of driving back to finish the job at another date. I'm not saying, go mow in the rain when it's thundering and lighting out. You gotta use your own judgment on that.

Yard maint: when you get a weed whacker I'd get one with a changeable head on it. That way you can buy the extra heads when you can afford them. You can get interchangeable heads for weed eating, edger, hedger, and tilling. Probably not going to need a tiller. But you never know. It depends on the demand. For a tiller, I'd get more of a heavy-duty one if you add tilling as part of your yard business. Preferably a tiller with the blade in the front. They're a bit better for seeing where you are going especially if your tilling to set up some concrete work. Rototilling can be a good side gig to your regular yard service.

Yard maintenance: to do a lot of yards, it would be good to set up groups of 2. Put one person doing a walk-through, picking up trash, taking pictures, and running the weed eater, and put the other one on the lawnmower. That works well for me and my crews. Both people get done about the same time. When you make enough money, you might invest in a riding mower and a push mower. It's nice to have both. You can expand quite a bit on lawn service. You'll get some standard rates through preservation work, and you might pick up some extra on the job.

General business: promotion is a big plus. Always have cards ready to hand out. If you are wanting to expand your preservation work, have cards and maybe a magnet sign on the side of your vehicle or trailer.

Initial cleaning or maid service: on an initial cleanout, you'll remove all the debris and clean out the house. See maid service checklist for what all needs done. One of the issues you'll find is getting water to do the cleaning. The water will usually be turned off. But if the property hasn't been winterized yet, you can get water out of the water heater or back of the toilet. Don't get it out of the front of the toilette, that would be gross. It's always a good idea to take two buckets with you for water and trash. I always took two 5 gallon jugs of water to help with maid services and flushing out toilets.

Cell Phone: a Cell phone is a must. This way you'll know you are not going to miss a job. If you get an emergency job or rush inspection, those usually pay a bit more. A cell phone with a photo app is essential.

Laptop: a laptop can be pretty handy so you can be on the road and load your information. This works well if you're working with a partner. While they drive, you can be downloading your information. That beats working for 10 to 16 hours, then getting home and having to put in another 4 hours logging your information and sending pictures.

Map sites: before you go somewhere, make sure you know where you are going. The google map has been a big help in finding places. GPS is another great tool. But they're not 100% especially if you have to inspect a property that's out in the country. Sometimes if you are going to an area that you are not too familiar with, it's a good idea to print out a copy of the property from the county assessor's website or go to their office and get one ran off. Sometimes to find a property, you may even have to go to the post office or call the police department.

If the property is a foreclosed property, there is usually a broker assigned to the property. Knowing which brokers specialize in foreclosed properties could help obtain more work. This could help with refurals for preservation work and possibly expand into remodeling projects.

http://maps.google.com/ www.bingmaps.com[1]

www.yellowpages.com[2]

---

1.   http://www.bingmaps.com

2.   http://www.yellowpages.com

Chapter 3
Tax preparation

As a business owner, it is essential that you keep track of all your expenses and money made. Most of the companies you contract with will send you a W9 to fill out and they'll send you a statement at the first of the year. For tax purposes, you'll need to keep records of:

- Mileage: you'll write down your beginning and ending mileage and each place or just the town you went to. Mileage can be a pretty good deduction.
- Expenditures: keep track of your expenditures, like buying a camera, batteries, tools. Make sure you get a receipt for everything.
- Money Made: any monies that you have made
- Office supply: this would expense on buying paper, pens, pencils, ink if you have to buy or replace a camera, computer fax machines,
- Advertisement
- Utilities: if you are running your business out of your home, you can dedicate a room for an office, and then you can deduct your utilities from your taxes. They usually deduct 10%.
- Equipment: This would be equipment that would devalue. Such as a riding lawn mower, push mower, air compressor, generator.... Etc
- Charge account: interest that you paid on charge accounts or credit cards would be a tax deduction.
- Cellphone expense
- Internet expense. This would include internet service and a website.

Mileage Log

Date Odometer Reading City

Date: _________________ Start: _____________________

City: _________________________________

Stop: _________________________________ City:

____

Date: _________________ Start: _____________________

City: _________________________________

Stop: _________________________________ City:

____

Date: _________________ Start: _____________________

City: _________________________________

Stop: _________________________________ City:

____

Date: _________________ Start: _____________________

City: _________________________________

Stop: _________________________________ City:

____

Date: _________________ Start: _____________________

City: _________________________________

Stop: _________________________________ City:

____

Date: _________________ Start: _____________________

City: _________________________________

Stop: _________________________________ City:

____

Date: _________________ Start: _____________________

City: _________________________________

Stop: _________________________________ City:

____

Date: ___________________   Start: _______________________________

City: ___________________________________

Stop: _______________________________   City:

____

Date: ___________________   Start: _______________________________

City: ___________________________________

Stop: _______________________________   City:

____

Total Miles: ___________________

Expenses
Date Item Reason cost

Total: ___________________

Money Made

Date Company Amount Made

Total: _______________________

Office Supplies

Date Item Reason cost

Total: _________________

Utilities

Month Gas Electric

January

February

March

April

May

June

July

August

September

October

November

December

Totals: ______________________________   ______________________________

Chapter 4
Property Management

Property Management

There are many ways to break into property management. If you are serious about an investment property or multifamily homes, for a first-time home buyer you can get a full loan to buy the property as long as it's going to be your primary residence. If you buy a multifamily house, I probably wouldn't say anything about renting any part of the house, because that may be considered more of a business loan, rather than a first home loan. If you're going more into a business loan or a loan specifically for an investment property, you may have to put in a 20% down payment. You could try an SBA or VA loan, but for a VA loan, you can't rent the property out until after 5 or 7 years. So if your looking at making the property into a rental property it might not be good to go that route.

On any property purchase, the first thing you get is the sheet from the county assessor's office and check any back taxes. That way you are prepared if there are a couple of years back taxes. If there are back taxes, have it written in the contract that upon payment of the property all taxes will be paid up to date and have that as part of the total cost of the property. If you are buying a multifamily dwelling that's been in business for quite some time, you would want to get their portfolio. So if you are going to get a business loan you have something to show what the property made. You would want a 3-year evaluation that would show the rental trends, consistency in rent, if there was a rent increase, how much each rental unit rents for per month, and you would want to have ready 3 years of taxes and maybe a business plan. A business plan example is on page 91.

There are many ways to obtain funds to buy a property. Personal loan, first homeowners loan, have the owner finance the property for you, do a lease to own. Maybe 10k down and so much a month. Or even credit cards. When I first started investing in investment property, I started with buying mobile homes. And you can pick them up for anywhere from $300 to $4500. Which is about the range for mobile home rental investments. You could buy a $50,000 mobile home, but it may take 30 years before you actually start making money off of that. You don't want to tie up your money that long. The other way is reading the newspaper in the classified, seeing what's for sale, and checking if there are any public auctions. Sometimes you can pick up property for cheap at a public auction. I spent $350 on a mobile home valued at $4500. I put $250 into the property and it was ready to rent. Made my money back within 2 months, rented it for 2 years, then sold it for $3500.

Investing in mobile homes can be a good and bad investment. You can pick them up cheap, put a couple thousand into the property, and a renter can tear it up in a month and ruin your entire investment. You get $400 rent and have to turn around and put another couple a thousand into it to get ready for the new renter. In wintertime, you have to worry about pipes freezing. So you set your winterization dates, start your checks on your mobile homes. Check to make sure your pipe heaters are working and that they are plugged in, and fix any skirting problems so you don't' have a cold air getting in.

Inspect your property. On the lease agreement, you would have written that you can give the notice to inspect the property within 24 hours with a notice or if the property looks like it's been vacant for 14 days. And it's good to do an inspection every few months to check smoke detectors (replace the batteries) and to check for any leaks. Check the ceilings for any leaks and check all faucets, and toilets for any leaks. That will help keep your property safe. Make sure you have working smoke detectors and are safe from water leaks that can cause wood rot and mold.

On diversified property management, there are several ways to expand on that. You can buy into an investment property, as well as contract with other investors that need help with management, as well as contract with realtors. Some realtors buy and sell property, but some will have a slue of rental properties all over. I do all. I own several investment properties. I contract with a couple of out-of-state investors that bought several apartments in my town, and I also work with a couple of realtors. The investors live about 250 miles away, the realtors live 60 miles away. When you have out-of-town investors, they need more help looking over their properties. But with the realtor, I also do basic repair, preservation work, and remodeling to help with their rental properties as well as help get the property to marketable condition. For working with realtors, you'll want to contact a realtor broker. They are the ones in charge and they'll cover a larger territory.

One way to promote and expand your business is you could look in the paper under the rental properties, and contact those people. You can go to the local chamber of commerce, who should have a list of landowners and rental property that you can contact. Or thumb through the yellow pages. I've had some recommended to me, and I've contacted apartment owners when I drive by an apartment complex that doesn't have good upkeep. You can check the unemployment office or even craigslist. I've found several leads off craigslist for property management as well as preservation work.

I dove into helping out an apartment owner that was having problems with the management and maintenance of one of their buildings. The manager wasn't responsible and the owner lived 250 miles away. This property was an 8 unit apartment that had only 3 units rented out. The other 5 had plumbing problems and nobody was paying rent. Don't get overwhelmed with something like that. When you take over as a manager or owner, you'll have to introduce yourself to the tenants and present them with what is expected. Most people want rent due on the 1st, but if someone is on SSI, they might not get a check until the 3rd or 7th. If they don't like your contract, they can find a different place to live. You should inspect each apartment and make a list of what needs to be done. What happened to the apartment that I took over management is that with the 3 renters that were there, one refused to pay rent, and they were evicted, the other person ended up going to jail for over 6 months for some fraud issue and she was evicted, the 3rd was the previous manager and I allowed him to stay. I started working on one apartment at a time, starting with the one that looked the easiest and quickest to get set up and ready to rent. Most of the plumbing was done wrong or half-assed. They were not hard fixes. They just needed to be fixed correctly. I got all units available to rent within 3 months, and kept the units at a minimum of 5 units filled. With the repairs, I did 90% of the work. And in rental properties, you want to do most of the work yourself. I did keep the old manager on for a year or two and that properties did go through a slue of pretty bad managers. Several were just taking a free ride with free rent and then didn't fix anything. The last manager was a drunk that would take 2 months to do a 3-hour job. He eventually ended up getting fired and evicted. As a rule of thumb, when someone moves out of a unit, you have 3 days to get it cleaned up and on the market. It should not take more time than that. This is how your turn and burn, and you keep the money coming in.

Page 84 shows an example of a property manager contract. I would suggest using something like that. Otherwise, you could be allowing free rent, then getting billed on every little job that the manager does. And you don't want to be billed extra for changing out a light bulb.

Property Manager Job Duties and Contract

Job Duties:

1. keep the premises in a fit and habitable condition.
2. Keep the common areas safe and sanitary.
3. Comply with building, housing, health, FHA, HUD, and safety codes.
4. Keep in good working order all electrical, plumbing, heating, and ventilation systems and fixtures.
5. Maintain all appliances and equipment supplied or required to be supplied by the landlord.
6. Provide running water and reasonable amounts of hot water and heat, unless the hot water and heat are supplied by an installation that is under the exclusive control of the tenant and supplied by a direct public utility hook-up.
7. Give at least 24 hours' notice, unless it is an emergency, before entering a tenant's unit, and enter only at reasonable times and in a reasonable manner.
8. Responsible for evictions for violators of the apartment lease agreements
9. Renting the units out to eligible tenants and making sure the lease is filled out correctly
10. General maintenance
11. Yard upkeep
12. Maintaining keys and locks to each unit and providing one key to new tenants
13. Collecting and depositing rent.
14. Informing owner of work that needs a contractor to do, except in emergencies
15. Total payment to the apartment manager is a minimum of

10% of the total money made from rental fees.

NOTE: This job description is not intended to be all-inclusive. Employees may perform other related duties as negotiated to meet the ongoing needs of the organization.

Signed: ________________________________   Date: ______________
Apartment Manager
     Signed: ________________________________ Date: ______________
Apartment owner

Property management tips:

- When you rent out a property you need to have a standard rental agreement that requires enough information that you can do a background check. A standard rental agreement is shown below.
- Always check references and never allow tenants to run on your utility account. Allowing tenants to run on your utility account can end up costing you a lot of money in the long run. Odds are, if the person that wants to rent your facility if they can't get the utilities transferred into their name, they probably can't afford your facility. They should utilize HUD housing and be a government burden rather than a private owner's burden.
- I'd watch out for people that are desperate to get into your building. Check the references to make sure they aren't skipping out of paying some other rent or utilities. If they skip out on paying rent on one landlord, odds are, they'll do it again. There is a lot of people that work the system where they will move into a place, pay the first month's rent, then

not pay for 2 or 3 months, they get evicted, they go to the next place and do the same thing. Pay one month, get 2 or 3 months free. But, you can always take those people to small claims court and garnish their wages or claim some of their property as payment.

- If the tenant is responsible for paying utilities, as soon as they sign that contract, I would suggest kicking off the breakers to the house. That way, they don't forget to switch the utilities over for 2 or 3 months.

- Have an account at a lumber yard and hardware store. They come in handy. Don't let tenants charge on your account. That is a big nono.

- When looking for buying property for rentals and you're having to get a loan from a bank, most will require a 20% down payment.

- For rental property, I would suggest going with a duplex or larger. Single houses can be tough. Good money when it is rented, but if you have a mortgage on the property and nobody lives there or they forget to pay rent for a couple of months, then you have to dig into your own pocket to pay that mortgage.

- When buying investment properties, this would be a building you would buy at a low cost, with high equity or you buy low, then you may invest $5,000 to $15,000 in remodeling to increase the equity to $50,000. Then you can barrow off that equity, up to $80 of the total appraised value of the house is standard. You can use that to improve the house or invest in another property.

- Equity: when investing in property you have to understand equity and whether or not a bank will loan out on that equity. What a bank will look at is what you have actually put into the property. If you get a property for free and its appraised value is $50,000, you still might not be able to get a loan off of that, because you don't have anything invested into it or you may be just asking the wrong bank. Something you can do is spend a couple thousand on remodeling, painting, maybe do some upgrading on plumbing, electric, or heating, then have the property appraised. Now you have an improvement, some money involved into the property and labor costs.

- On maintenance, if you are not doing at least 80% of your maintenance, odds are you'll run over budget all the time. You need to be doing at least 80% of your maintenance. If you hire a manager, I'd recommend hiring someone that has some general maintenance skills.

- If you see rental properties that are not being maintained, that might be opportunities. Maybe they are looking for a manager or maintenance person, or maybe even sell out. You could add that housing complex to your regular route.

- If you're doing preservation work, that might be a way to have an insider on an upcoming investment property.

- The number one thing you do before purchasing a property is to check with the county assessor's office and get their rip sheet on that property and check the taxes and see if there are any back taxes. You don't want to be surprised with buying a property and then having to spend a ton of money for back taxes. I bought into a $500k investment property for $50,000. Was a pretty good deal, I knew it had a few years back taxes, which was alright. I was still coming out quite a bit ahead. After I signed the contract, in that same month an asset company bought out the taxes, which put that property in flux for 8 months until it went through the courts, and the asset company settled on a price to buy out the taxes. They paid $6400 in taxes and tacked on 14% to that which rounded up to $12,000.

- Receiving rent payments. Most will pay with cash, but nowadays there are several ways you can get your rent payments. Checks and money orders are alright, but with a check, people can bounce those, and you may be out of that cash for a month or two, or they may never pay you back. You can set up a website for your rental property and have online payment. Doing online payments you could set up a PayPal account and set up a "pay it now" button and people can pay their rent using Paypal or as a guess using a credit card. Or you can use a square. A devise that hooks into your cell phone and tenants can pay with their credit card that way.

Residential Lease Agreement

1. Identification of Landlord and Tenant:

This Agreement is entered into on ____________ between ______________________________ and ________________________________("Tenant") and ___________________ ("Landlord")

1. Address of Property

Subject to the terms and conditions in this Agreement, Landlord rents to Tenant, and Tenant rents from Landlord, for residential purposes only, the premises located at ___________________Alliance, NE. ("The premises"), together with the following furnishings and appliances:

____

1. Limits on Use and Occupancy

The premises are to be used only as a private residence for Tenants listed in 1.

Occupancy by a guest for more than 14 days is prohibited without Landlord's written consent and will be a breach of this Agreement.

1. Term of the Tenancy:

The term of the rental will begin on ____________, and end on __________, 20__.

If the Tenant vacates before the term ends Tenant will be liable for the balance of the rent for the remainder of the term.

1. Payment of Rent:

Tenant will pay to Landlord a monthly rent of

__________________________________**dollars**,

payable in advance by the 1st day of each month, except when

that day falls on a weekend or legal holiday, in which case the rent

is due on the next business day. Rent checks or money orders will

be written out to _______________________ **Land Lord. ”**.

There will be a _____________________________ Address that all

rent checks will need to be delivered to. A late charge of $25

will be addressed when the rent money is not received by the

seventh day of the month by 5 pm. $50 for the second month

and eviction will be mandatory if you are late the third month

unless otherwise notified. A $40 fee will be charged for returned

checks.

1. Security Deposit:

On signing this Agreement, the Tenant will pay to Landlord the sum of $ _________ as a security deposit of which $50.00 is none refundable. A tenant may not, without Landlord's prior written consent, apply this security deposit to the last month's rent or any other sum due under this agreement. Within 45 days after Tenant has vacated the premises, returned keys, and provided Landlord with a forwarding address, Landlord will give Tenant an itemized list written statement of the reasons for, and the dollar amount of, any of the security deposit retained by the Landlord, along with a check for any deposit balance. The landlord reserves the right to apply the security deposit to any amounts due, including any rent outstanding and late charges.

1. Utilities:

The tenant will pay all utility charges.

Must provide proof that electricity and gas has been transferred over to tenants name before receiving keys

1. Assignment and Subletting:

The tenant will not sublet any part of the premises or assign this Agreement without the prior written consent of the Landlord.

1. Tenants maintenance Responsibilities:

Tenant will: (1.) Keep the premises clean and in good condition and, upon the termination of the tenancy, return the premises to the Landlord in a condition identical to that which existed when Tenant took occupancy, except for ordinary wear and tear. (2.) Immediately notify Landlord of any defects or dangerous conditions in and about the premises of which tenant becomes aware, and (3.) reimburse Landlord, on-demand by Landlord, for the cost of any repairs to the premises damaged by Tenant or Tenant's guest or business invitees through misuse or neglect.

The tenant has examined the premises, including appliances, fixtures, carpet, and paint, and has found them to be in good, safe and clean condition and repair, except as noted below.

1. **Repairs and Alterations by Tenant**
    A. **Except as provided by law, as authorized below or by the prior written consent of the Landlord, the Tenant will not make any repairs or alterations to the premises.**
    B. **Tenant will not, without Landlord's prior written consent, alter, re-key, or install locks to the premises or install or alter any burglar alarm system. Tenant will provide Landlord with a key or keys capable of unlocking all such re-keyed or new locks as well as for instructions on how to disarm and alter or new burglar alarm system.**

1. **Violating Laws and Causing Disturbances:**

The tenant is entitled to quiet enjoyment of the premises. Tenants and guests or invitees will not use the premises or adjacent areas in such a way as to, **(1)** violate any law or ordinance including laws prohibiting the use, possession, or sale of illegal drugs. **(2)** Commit waste (severe property damage); or **(3)** create a nuisance by annoying, disturbing, inconveniencing, or interfering with the quiet enjoyment and peace and quiet of any other tenant or nearby residents

1. Pet Policy:

No animal, bird, or other pet will be kept on the premises, except properly trained dogs needed by blind, deaf or disabled persons, except as expressly permitted in writing by Landlord. Any pets expressly allowed by the Landlord will be required to be properly restrained at all times, in accordance with Park rules and all local rules and regulations. Any pets will also be required to be properly vaccinated and licensed. An additional deposit of $25.00 (twenty-five dollars) will be required to be reserved for any and all damages caused to the property by the keeping of pets on the property. No more than 2 pets are allowed. No more than 1 dog is allowed.

1. Landlord's Right to Access:

Landlord or Landlord's agents may enter the premises in the event of an emergency, to make repairs or improvements or to show the premises to prospective buyers or tenants. A landlord may also enter the premises to conduct an annual inspection to check for safety or maintenance problems. Except in cases of emergency, Tenant's abandonment of the premises, court order, or where it is impractical to do so, the landlord shall give Tenant 24 hours notice before entering.

1. Extended absences by Tenant:

The tenant will notify Landlord in advance if the Tenant will be away from the premises for 7 or more consecutive days. During such absence, the Landlord may enter the premises at times reasonably necessary to maintain their property and inspect for needed repairs.

1. Possession of the premises:

A. Tenant's failure to take possession.

If, after signing this agreement, the Tenant fails to take possession of the premises, Tenant will still be responsible for paying rent and complying with all other terms of this agreement.

A. Landlord's failure to deliver possession.

If Landlord control, including, but not limited to, partial or complete destruction of the Premises, Tenant will have the right to terminate this Agreement upon proper notice as required by law. In such an event, Landlord's Liability to Tenant will be limited to the return of all sums previously paid by Tenant to Landlord.

1. Disclosure:

Tenant acknowledges that Landlord has made the following disclosures regarding the premises:

Disclosure of information on Lead-based Paint and/or Lead-Based Paint Hazards

1. Grounds for Termination of Tenancy:

The failure of Tenant or Tenant's guests or invitees to comply with any term of this agreement, or the misrepresentation of any material fact on Tenant's Rental Application, are grounds for termination of the tenancy, with appropriate notice to tenants and procedures as required by law. Either party may terminate this lease with a 30-day notice after the term stated in paragraph 4

1. Entire Agreement:
      A. This document constitutes the entire Agreement between the parties, and no promises or other representations, other than those contained here and those implied by law, have been made by the

Landlord and Tenant.

B. The failure of the Tenant or their guests or invitees to comply with any term of this Agreement are grounds for termination of the tenancy, with appropriate notice to tenants and procedures as required by law.

Date _______________________

Scott Bolinger (President of Bolinger & Associates)

Signature: _________________________________

Street Address : _______________

City, State & Zip : ___________________________

Phone : __________________

Date ____

Tenant   ____

____

Print

Signature: ____

____

Phone# ____

Cell#: ____

Social Security Number _______________________

Drivers License Number: _______________________

<u>**References: (name, address, phone number) Former Landlord :**</u>

Name: _______________________________ Phone Number:

____

Name: ______________________________________ Phone Number:
____

Name: ______________________________________ Phone Number:
____

Former Landlord: _________________________________ Phone
Number: _______________________

Place of Employment: ______________________________ Phone
Number: _______________________

Example Business Plan

Central Estates

business plan
by
Scott Bolinger

Written by Scott Bolinger, owner of Central Estates and Bolinger & Associates

Introduction:

I've been a business owner since 1998, starting in network marketing, then expanding into investment properties, stocks, field inspections, and Property Preservation work. Started from scratch and built up to a net worth of over $500,000.

Type of business:

The central estates will be located at 715 Box Butte. It has 24 rooms. I plan to create studio apartments in 15 rooms. The larger rooms may be set up as fully furnished with utilities, while the smaller rooms may be catered to the railroad, barrow-outs, harvest crews, or college students. The rooms can be modified to meet the rental demand, if someone wants a one-bedroom, up to a 3 bedroom and in some cases may cater to their building specs. There will also be a gym for personal use for residence. Eventually, I will allow public use of the gym.

Market Demand:

At this time, there is a shortage of rental property. I've been in the rental property business for over 11 years, and I get several calls a day from people looking for property to rent.

Start-up costs:

✓ The total cost of the building $50,000 has been paid in full.

✓ Liability insurance $1200

✓ Building insurance $2200

✓ $3000 to $5000 per room for restructuring for the 1st and 2nd floor. May go more elaborate for the 3rd floor. The first plan is to get the 1st and 2nd floor rented out first.

✓ Gym equipment: already have $10,000 in equipment

✓ Office supplies: have in stock already

✓ General maintenance per month: $200

✓ Water per month: $200

✓ Preservation equipment: already have $20,000 in equipment and supplies. Costs roughly $200 a month to keep in supplies

✓ Water main repair will cost between $500 to $3000

✓ Install meters and heating/cooling units per apartment: $700

✓ Install tankless water heater for kitchen and bathroom. $300. I have one in stock.

✓ Monthly building payments $ .00

✓ Monthly tax payment $200

Primary projects:

✓ Fix water main: cost is between $1500 and $3000

✓ Secure water lines and section off 3rd floor: estimated cost $1500

✓ Install tankless water heater in the kitchen: estimated cost $300 (already in stock)

✓ Make sure there is running water in the kitchen and bathroom off the gym, then expand into the other bathrooms.

✓ Find a buyer for the boiler system, or scrap it out (quote from scrapping the boiler system would bring in $8000)

✓ File for LLC (in the process as of August 2013)

✓ File for historical building

✓ Construct rain catcher with gravity irrigation (in the process)

Projection:

The first thing would be to set up 5 rooms fully furnished. I have most of the furnishings to do this already. Rent at $525 would create $2625 a month. Then the rest would be un-furnished. 10 rooms at $425 a month would bring in another $4250 with a total of $6875. The primary thing is to get the 5 rooms rented out quickly, and that will pay for the building and general maintenance, as well as allow extra income for expansions. This will also allow a live-in maintenance position.

The first stage (first month)

✓ Replace main water valve and have running water in the bathroom off of gym and in the kitchen

✓ Install a new water heater

✓ Set up living quarters for maintenance person and add a heating / cooling unit

✓ Fix windows

✓ Get rid of graffiti

✓ Have inspection for occupancy approval

The second stage (By Month 8) Income is $2125 a month. 8% goes to the maintenance person.

✓ Set up 5 rooms for rental units
✓ Each room will be on its own electric meter
✓ These rooms will be set up as studio (boarding house) settings
✓ Install laundry room with vending machines
✓ Set up a picnic area
✓ Expand on rain catcher and irrigation project

Third stage (By Month 16) Income $4250 a month. 8% goes to the maintenance person.

✓ Add 5 more units for boarding house

✓ Take out old boiler system and set up general maintenance area in boiler area.

✓ Set up 2 more bathrooms and shower area

✓ Add double fire-rated door between the residential units and gym. Replace wood doors with metal doors. And set up a budget to get the gym up to code for public use.

✓ Upgrade fire alarm system

Fourth Stage (By Month 24) Income $6875 a month. 8% goes to the maintenance person.

✓ Add 5 units that are self-contained with their own bathroom and kitchen
✓ Expand washroom
✓ Budget to expand parking area on Northside
✓

Fifth Stage (By Month 36)

✓ Convert 5 boarding house units to self-contained units

✓ First, parking area expansion completed

✓ Budget to replate east open lot to install residential units for senior assisted living.

✓ Set budget to expand second parking expansion on the east and west sides.

Price list:

$425 boarding house setting
$525 self-contained

+ $100 to add a 10x20 room

BunkHouse

Cost to complete

$400 to construct partitions

Furniture, already have in stock

Couch, tv, refrigerator, microwave, already have in stock

$300 Build cabinet for kitchen

$120 sink

$200 run water and drain lines for the sink

Bathroom (will use community bath)

Penthouse Apartment

    This is the manager's residence

    This would rent for $750

    The two large rooms are 20x30 and the two small rooms are 10x20

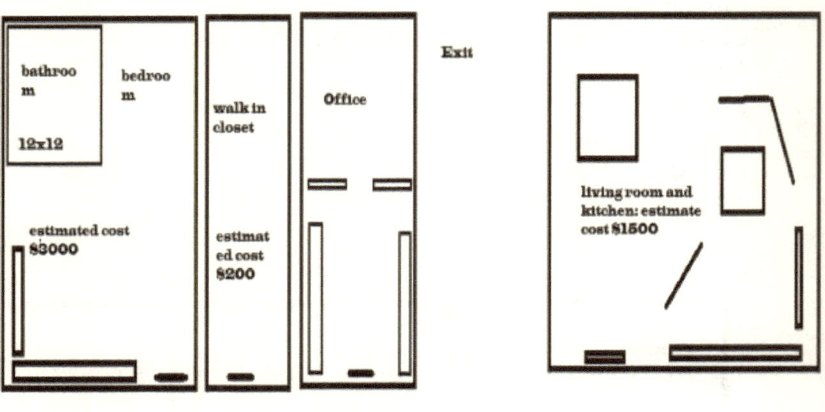

Penthouse Apartment

Single Room Apartment

Rent on this one-bedroom will be $425

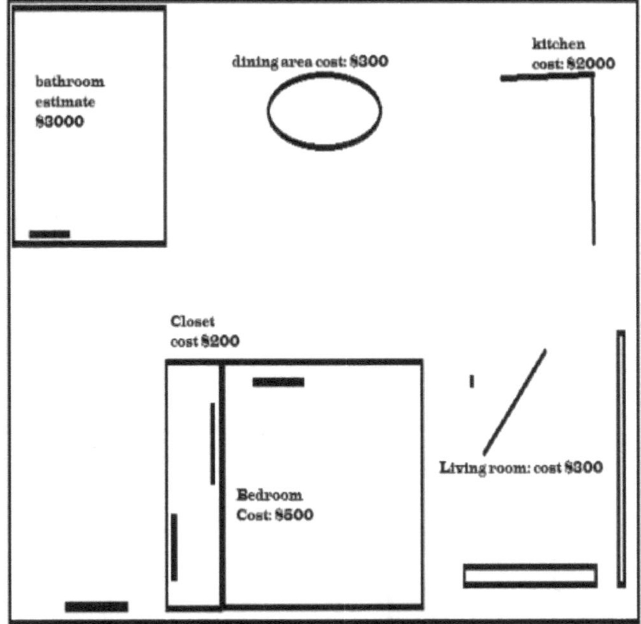

Two Bedroom

This two-bedroom would rent for $475

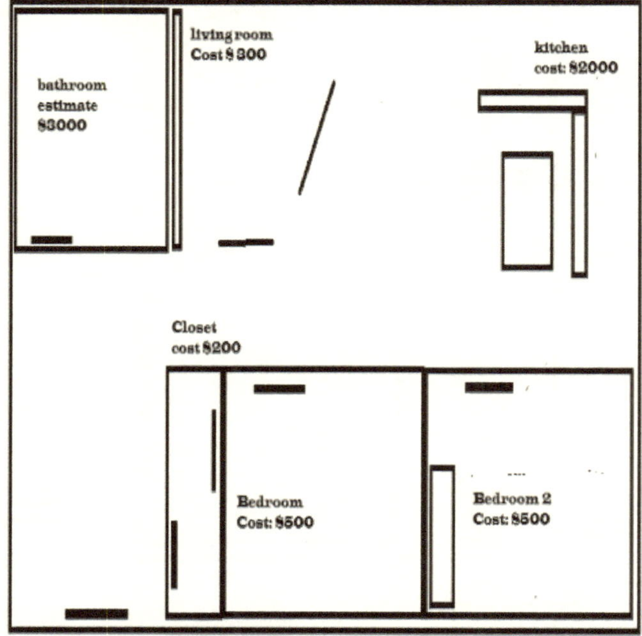

Chapter 5
Politics

Bolinger in Politics

I have run for public office for many years and I have tried to push different agendas to better our housing problems. In 2018 I ran for Congress dist. 3 as a Republican in Nebraska. I was also a candidate in the 2020 election period. In 2022 I decided to run for Attorney General after I obtained a Bachelor of Science degree. The things that I'm trying to improve are our school security with my self-defense and restraint book, improving the farm bill, improving the school lunch bill, securing social security, expanding Medicaid, and improving the housing market. What I would like to accomplish with this book is to expand it well enough to help both the housing market and increase work for contractors.

In this chapter, I go through several research analyses that I have done. Some of the information I have sent to elected representatives to help create positive changes in the housing and contractor business.

HUD housing approval:

While running for the 2018 congressional seat one of my supporters wanted me to bring up an issue of HUD housing assistance. Where if you have approval for assistance for a mobile home, but that assistance did not cover the lot rent. He wanted the HUD assistant to cover both. The thing is with renting a mobile home, land rent is something that is usually done, so it is odd that the land rent was not counted towards the total rental of the property. So on this, I start with sending out a request to the state legislature to try and gain some interests to push to the HUD department and if I can't get the interests, then I go to the state HUD department directly, then the federal department. But, the person did have a point where both should be covered as both the mobile home and lot rent are needed for rent to be able to live there. But if the person owns the mobile home, and is approved for housing assistance, then the lot rent should be claimed as a rent expense.

Foreclosure Reform Bill Requests:

Foreclosure Reform

By

Larry Bolinger

This is a bill that I have preproposals several times in the past 4 years. This is a bill that could reduce at least 70% of the foreclosures in the state:

I've been in the property preservation business for years and it's a bit of a rat race. What I've seen is when a property is foreclosed on, or goes into bankruptcy, and even on a reverse mortgage, that property could sit for 2 or 3 years before it gets put on the market to sell. Even if a property owner volunteers to give up his rights to that property, the property still might sit for a year before it's put up for sale. Having a property sit for a couple of years at a time before being put up for market may deteriorate the building. And with the current contracting, a bank or broker might contract or is forced to contract with national property preservation companies who I've seen work in a very unethical manner in a way that could be argued as labor law violations. Where they may have a standard on initial service then cutting contractor prices, creating back-charges, or when faced with legal issues instead of taking responsibility, those corporations change their business name close their business and bump everything to their secondary business which clears them of any legal issues and then they continue the business. Property preservation can be a cut-throat business. Every company is trying to undercut the other to obtain contracts, and then send out inspections to support not paying contractors, back charging contractors for work that a contractor wasn't assigned to do, or charging contractors for late work. There is a standard HuD pay out that is already in place and that's what every PP or REO company should be going on, rather than billing the bank the standard cost, then turning around and taking 40% to 60% off the top before you pay the contractors and expect more and more work out of them for less and less pay. The standard deduction is 20%, but companies that get the bigger contracts take more than the standard. And what I've seen, is a national company creating other sister companies to them, so if they have to close one company due to unethical business practices, then they have one of their other

companies take over. And I've seen it where they create a company, umbrella the company, then have their umbrella company take over the work orders and cut contractor wages.

If there was a direct contract with the broker as the coordinator of PP and REO work and billed out to the banks directly you would get rid of the low unethical wages given to the contractors. The Realty Brokers could hire out QC / Processing companies to manage the work progress. This could push for more contractor work for local contractors.

What I'd like to see, is when a property has to go to foreclosure, that the land owner can contract with a broker to sell the property. And when the land owner does that, it safeguards the property from being foreclosed and stops the full takeover by the bank. The property being marketed would have to be brought up to FHA standard, and there would continue to be a need for a Property Preservation specialist to get the property up to FHA code and in sellable condition.

The change I propose is annexing the current system. What I'd like to see, instead of empowering one company in the state to take people's property and be the sole company making money off this deal, that if a property is in a position to be foreclosed, or tax lien fore closed and has to be sold that the owner would have an opportunity to contract with a broker to sale the property and be given adequate time to get the property sold. I would suggest a 3-year term for sale. Most properties sell at 3 months. For the sale of a property, you would still have to get the property up to FHA reg.. which would mean to continue the hiring of property preservation specialists to bring the property up to FHA regs. , the standard cost for getting a property cleaned up, and up to FHA regs varies, usually between $750 and $1500, but a good standard for an allowable cost is $5000. Empowering the brokers to safeguard these properties will help get them listed within weeks rather than with the current system which could take years. And instead, thousands of people lose their property and homes due to foreclosure and tax lien forecloses and asset companies taking advantage of that, to where a small few are making money off people miss-fortune, you put the power to the broker to safe guard those properties and help those thousands of people and banks to settle a debt. Getting a property to market quicker, sold, taxes paid up to date, any liens paid off, and banks and brokers paid, with the possibility that the property owner would get relieved of debt and maybe make some extra cash.

Fighting the Banks

As of 2021, I have had over 20 years of experience as a contractor and 13 years of experience in the property preservation business. In the "Property Preservation" business I contracted with roughly 20 different national companies from all over the U.S. Those companies contract with banks and brokers. I've seen the ups and downs of the business. Over the past several years there have been trends in the business. These trends created issues of the banks and national companies cutting wages, creating penalties towards contractors, and refusing to pay for completed work. I remember one year that one of the companies that I was contracted for mismanaged the pay so bad that I was short almost

$20,000. In a contracting business half of your money might be going towards supplies and employees. I was supposed to have made $45,000 that year, but the company skimmed almost half my money. In this instant, I was a sub-contractor to a sub-contracting business that contracted with MSN that worked on HuD foreclosed properties. I got paid half my wages and the person that skimmed the money was able to get a new swimming pool and take a trip to the Caribbean. MSN has a lien waiver contract. So you as a contractor waive your rights to lean if the company denies you pay. They threaten that if you file a lien they will charge you $50,000. Many contractors lost a great deal more money than I had lost. I had conducted a research analysis and wrote policy request changes. I had written to several Senators and to the local city council to help push the policy to the Legislature. This chapter will follow some of the conversations I have had with City Council members and to my district Legislature representative and it will have the research analysis that I conducted.

Letter to Tom Brewer (Nebraska State Legislature) 3/20/2017

Hello

My name is Larry Bolinger

I'm a veteran and republican voter. I did vote for you in the last election.

I'm writing to you today in concern of a program that I've been involved in for about 10 years concerning the property management and property preservation business which consist of working with HUD, FHA, Banks, Property Management companies, and realty brokers with the business of working on foreclosed properties.

There are several bills that I'd like to try and push that concern how property management is being done through the banks, HUD, and property management businesses. For the past 3 or 4 years, the whole system has been a big mess. Brokers, property management companies and HUD have taken advantage of the contractors that do the actual work. In many ways, they have taken advantage of contractors and subcontractors. I believe we need to update or create some new laws, new bills to protect the contractors doing the work.

Lien Waiver: the first bill would be to make a law that takes away a corporation's ability to make subcontractors or contractors sign a waiver, waiving their rights to lien. In many states, you can't waive someone's rights. In Nebraska, you can waive your rights. Waiving your rights away results in you having to fight tooth and nail to get your money or you just end up working on no pay.

I would like to see mechanical liens changed from 90 days to being able to file a mechanical lien up to one year after the job is completed. Many Banks or contracting companies that work with banks may not pay within 90 days as a standard pay practice.

By forcing contractors to sign lien waivers it gives the banking industry, the contract hiring companies, and realtor/brokers a lot of pole over a contractor. It gives them the ability to manipulate the pay. Many issues that come up regularly are after a debris removal is completed. The bank contracting company will cut half the total cubic yard and reduce the price to the contractor by half. I have gone out, taken pictures, made a bid on the total cubic yard, got approval for the pay and total cubic yard, got the job done, then the cyrds yard and pay was cut in half. I had the bid approved for the job and the job was done correctly. After the job was completed the company cut the payout.

There were times where an "Initial clean out" was done and the job was cut or refused pay. That type of job consists of an initial yard service, debris removal, and initial maid service. Some businesses have a standard rate of $750 for that particular job. Bank contracting (Field Asset Services) companies have been known to refuse to pay because of a small error such as a missing photo such as a picture of moping the floor even though it was obvious that the floor was mopped. Another similar case, the same type of worker order with about a $750 payout. The contracting company (SafeGuard Properties) refused to pay because one air freshener picture was blurry. Another payout issue, similar payout, the contracting company refused to pay out because they wanted a set of finishing pictures. Finishing pictures were sent to the regional manager's email 10 times because the contracting company's website was not working right. The contracting company refused to pay and I had to put a mechanical lien on the property. They ended up paying but I had to sign an agreement to never work for that company again. That company was "SafeGuard" which does the majority of the HUD contracts.

I had an issue with a company that was skimming money from a lot of work orders. A company called MCS. I thought I was being shorted and that they would eventually catch up on the pay. End up going over 6 months' worth of work orders and found many work order prices were cut in half. And some work was marked with a zero payout and over 50 work orders not paid which totaled to over $10,000. And they are refusing to pay. On a mechanical lien, you have to file the lien within 90 days after the work has been completed. If you're a subcontractor that signed the lien waiver it states in that contract that the contracting company can sue you for $50,000. You are basically set up to be hosed. If you're a sub of a subcontractor, it's a total loss.

Another big trend. Wellsfargo started fining inspectors if they inspect a property and there isn't a Wellsfargo window sign in a window. They will charge the inspector $250. The inspection itself pays out $8 and the bank is going to charge them $250 if they don't put a tag on the window or if they put the wrong tag on the window.

A big trend over the past few years is contracting companies looking for any reason to create a back charge. Any late work might not get paid and contractors could be back charged on top of not being paid. The bank gets the job done and then charges the contractors. I had one company that did that quite a lot. There were so many back charges from the inspections that it was taking half my contractor pay. So I had to go back and review the entire year, and there were many back chargers for a late inspection. But the inspections were sent in and completed.

Another big trend is large corporations employing organizations to higher subcontractors. Doing your hiring done this way, the main cooperation gets out of having to pay a high insurance or workman's comp. Subcontractors are independent contractors that have to have their own license, insurance, and sometimes E&0 insurance. Rail Road, some store chains, and banks higher organizations to hire out subcontractors.

The preservation contractors usually have to file to get their background checks then they have to do background checks on their own company. In some cases, they have to have a contractor license and at least general liability insurance. But over the past year or so, more and more companies are wanting the contractors to have insurance through only one of 3 companies, which are

York–Jersey   800-392-6958   http://www.york-jersey.com/mortgages.html

Leonard 800-451-1904 http://www.leonardinsurance.com/page/property-preservation-insurance

Brunswick   800-686-8080 https://www.brunswickcompanies.com/property-preservation/

By changing insurance companies makes my insurance prices go from $750 per year to roughly $5100 per year.

Another issue on insurance is the bank contracting company. Many of them want you to add them to your insurance. Usually, you have to send them a certificate of insurance, which is pretty standard. But some want you to add them to your insurance. Which by doing so gives them rights to make claims on your account. Which has happed to me by a company called AMS. AMS is a contracting company for Fanney Mae. They made a false claim to my insurance company on a work order that I didn't do and I fought it for two years. But, shortly after AMS made that false claim and got paid they closed the AMS business and transferred it into their sister business Guardian Asset Management and Asserio. That is a standard business practice. When someone claims a suit against your company you simply bankrupt and close its doors and transfer everything to a sister business and you don't skip a beat.

One of the biggest scams of these banking contract companies is they'll run several different companies. One as their primary business and then one or two of those companies are used as their dump-offs. That way they can get several bids and then get other bids from their 2 or 3 different companies to meet the minimum bids to get approval. Now, if they mess up a lot and are looking at a possible lawsuit all they have to do to prevent losing any money is to just close up shop and dump off to their secondary companies.

What I'd like to see done in a Bill is to make it illegal for cooperation to force contractors into signing a waiver to be able to do work for them. I would also like to see it made illegal for these companies to force contractors to get insurance for a company of their choosing. That should be the contractor or sub-contractors decision. I can see setting a million or 2 million minimum coverage, but that's should be the only demand. I would also like to see it made illegal for these companies to create back charges to get out of paying contractors full pay.

On top of these bills, I would also request an investigation into these bank contracting companies, starting with every company that has a direct contract with Fannie Mae, which would also include Fannie Maes's preservation department.

A secondary bill to this would be on a mechanical lien time limit. I would want the time limit increased. Letts start protecting the contractors.

Mechanical liens: In most states, you have to file the mechanical lien within 90 days of completing the job. For a preservation specialist that works with banks and brokers, many of these companies, instead of paying out within 2 to 3 weeks like they used to had changed to a 45 / 90 tic. Which you get paid in 45 to 90 days, usually there is an error that will easily push that 45 days to extend another month without pay so most checks or at least most large checks are pushed past the 90-day mark. So you are forced to take whatever pay they want to pay and usually with a significant cut in a negotiated price. One company I worked for would review the work you did a month after you did the work. If the work is approved, the payment will be done the next month. Most of the time the work is not approved. It will always need something even if everything is done. By doing that, the work order has to wait an additional month before it is reviewed again and might be approved. If it gets approved that time the payout will be a month after that. So the payout is 3 months past the actual time the work was completed. Banks are real prose at milking the pay and cutting the price. And some cut the price so bad they charge a back charge so a contractor could do the work, get a back charge and have to pay. That's borderline slave labor. So I propose to extend the mechanical lien to 1 year to get banks away from milking the pay. Make it law that at least our government-owned banks payout within 3 weeks of the job completion. If a national management company is holding paychecks they should be fined and/or lose their contracts.

Contractor preservation bill: I would like to see a bill that would force banks to pay contractors/subcontractors their earned income within 3 weeks. If they have a contracted management company, that management company will have 3 weeks to pay the contractors or they receive a fine or lose their contract with that bank. Many property management companies went from a 3-week payout to 45 to 90 days, which in many cases turns into a 3 to 6 month pay period. What does happen is if a contractor cannot get the job done in an allowable time. The management company decreases their pay or even back charges the contractor for late work. Usually, any contract job is allowed 3 days to complete unless it is an emergency. Emergency needs to have a response within 24 hours. But if the contractor isn't getting paid in a reasonable time frame it gets very tough for the contractor to run a smooth well-oiled business. If payment is done regularly then the contractors can be consistent in the work they do. Keep the contractors regularly paid at a reasonable pay rate, properties get repaired and managed to meet FHA regulations and in a conveyance or saleable condition which will intern makes a faster house turn around. In many cases where banks don't pay out for 45 to 90 days, the contractors end up running out of money to continue the work. So they have to shut down. Then the managing company has to find another contractor to continue work. Sometimes work is lost or a contractor cancels the contract. I've seen management company's jump from one contractor to another contractor to another contractor. Every couple of month they change the contractor because the management company cuts the agreed payments in half, refuse to pay, or take too long to pay. Instead of paying the contractors they just move on to someone else. And there is no way of making these banks or property management companies held accountable. At the least, we should be able to create a law that forces the federally owned banks to pay contractors within those 3 weeks. That would force the federally owned bank like Fanny Mae, Freddy Mac, and Ginnie Mae to do a 3-week payout for all preservation work.

Resent on 7/7/2017

Tony Baker <tbaker@leg.ne.gov>   11:19 AM (2 hours ago)

to me

Hello Larry,

Thanks for your extensive note. You've done a lot of homework here. The issues you raise are definitely worth a piece of legislation. Now you need to find a senator to "carry your bill."

That said, Sen. Brewer doesn't have anymore room on his plate.

"Legislatures" in Nebraska run two years. This "first" session of the 105th Legislature was last January-April. The "second" session of the 105th Legislature will be next January-March.

We introduced 13 bills last session. One was signed into law. One was advanced to general file and never put on the calendar, and the rest are stuck "held in committee." We have one which is the subject of an interim study which means it will likely pass into law. We're trying to amend a few of our bills to try and help them out of committee. I'm reasonably sure most of the other senators are in the same boat.

Bottomline, we can't carry it. Even if we could write and introduce this, Sen. Brewer has already pledged his one "priority bill" status to another measure. Without this being a "priority bill" (every senator gets one) there is almost no way this will get out of committee in the next session.

Do not lose heart.

Polish this. Get it to the point it can be handed to a bill drafter and actually turned into a bill. Develop a constituency of people willing to help, write letters, testify at a hearing, call/visit/lobby senators, etc.

A bill about this stuff would probably go in front of the Business and Labor Committee. The committee chairman gets two priority bills. Contact the members of this committee. See if one of them will carry/prioritize a bill like this. Schedule a meeting with the chairman. Put together a presentation for her. See if she might use a committee priority on a bill like this.

See: http://news.legislature.ne.gov/bui/

Sending Sen. Brewer this note was the BEGINNING of the remedy you seek.

Much remains to be done. Stay in touch. I will help you navigate this process. It's a "gub'mint" process after all so it's not complicated, just tedious.

Sincerely,

Tony D. Baker

Legislative Aide

Sen. Tom Brewer, 43rd Legislative District

402-471-2628 / 2606

tbaker@leg.ne.gov

http://www.nebraskalegislature.gov/

The argument of the Property Preservations pay and refusal to pay and the penalties are constitutional violations of the 14th amendment of life, liberty, and property without a due process of law. They would have to have due process before any penalties could be done. These labor violations could be a form of slave labor. I have fought to make changes in policies but the same people get elected into office so policies don't change for the better. Federal-owned banks have argued that since they are federally owned a contractor cannot file suit against them. But one can argue that since they claim to be the federal government they have to be held accountable to constitutional proceedings. Which is the contractors cannot be penalized without due process of law.

I decided to write a request to the city manager and city council to try and gain support from them to make a push to the legislature to make changes in policies. I also tried to get them to present this to the League of Municipalities to try and gain support to utilize them in putting pressure on the Legislature.

21 May 2017

Note to the city manager and council concerning bank-owned and foreclosed houses

Hello

This is Scott Bolinger

I wanted to send out this message to the city manager and city council.

It's basically concerning the abandoned, bank-owned, and realtor-owned properties. These are usually foreclosed homes or homes obtained in bankruptcy that are supposed to be maintained by the banks and brokers. This is something that I have talked to with a couple of city council, police officers, and code enforcement officers. Most of these properties are not being taken care of. Banks hire out national contracting companies to take care of these properties and bring them up to the FHA code and bring them into compliance to be able to be sold. Roughly 90% of the properties sold by banks and brokers are not meeting FHA code. 3 years ago, they were within code, but for the past 3 years, the banks have not been maintaining the properties like they are supposed to. I did express that if the city pushed a little they could get these banks and national contracting businesses to actually do what they are supposed to and start taking care of these houses. It doesn't take much of a push. When a property doesn't meet city code, a simple notice on the door helps out. Try calling if you can, but also put up a door tag. There are usually inspectors and brokers that inspect the foreclosed properties at least twice a month. By keeping these properties maintained could bring in between $50,000 - $300,000 in contract work. If we had a working broker in town the expansion of preservation work would be significant. As of right now, the majority of the broker contracts are between 2 brokers that cover the region. Those two brokers are based out of Scottsbluff. If Alliance had brokers that worked with the banks they could retain those. Keeping the money in-house rather than towards another city will help our economy.

The excuse I received from the city workers is that you can hardly get a hold of the banks or the contracted company and that it was a big waste of time doing anything because nothing gets done. It is not difficult to get these properties maintained. It would bring in more work and more jobs but you have to be willing to do the job and have a little bit of knowledge of how foreclosed, bank-owned, and realty owned properties are handled and know the HUD/FHA codes. I've been handling these types of properties for over 10. I wrote to the city manager and stated that "if you give me the code enforcement contract, I can get these properties maintained and bring income into this town."

note: This information was sent to the city clerk and city manager then I waited 2 months and sent the messages to the city council.

Email to Posha Gonzalas (city council)

I wrote a couple of times to Linda Jines, which the message was supposed to go to the city manager for review about the abandoned and foreclosed property. And I have yet to get any callback or email about this. They as well as the rest of the city management don't know the process and how to make that process work better for Alliance and I do. I've been in the business for over 10 years. And right now by not getting the correct actions done most of the work is given to contractors and brokers in Scottsbluff and Omaha.

Linda Jines (City Clerk)

Mr. Bolinger –

I am in receipt of your e-mail dated May 21, 2017. I have forwarded the information as requested. Thank you for your suggestions on how to handle bank-owned/handled property.

Alliance has a City Manager form of government which requires all personnel matters to be addressed with the City Manager.

Note: this particular issue wasn't a personal matter. This was an unethical business practice that has been allowed across the nation. Jines has claimed things as personal matters so that she has an excuse not to pass along my messages to the City Council. This obviously was an issue that needed to be presented to lawmakers. It is something that could not be fixed by a city clerk or manager. Some of the code enforcement procedures could be fixed by the city manager. But official policy changes would have to come from the City Council and State Legislature.

to Linda

No one got back in contact with me about these distressed bank-owned and broker-owned properties.

Posha (City council):

That is presumptuous on your part to make that judgment on me. And I will say it back to you—Scott- there are a lot of things you don't understand about how the City works and what regulations and statutes need to be followed.

If you want to pursue this issue, then you are welcome to schedule a meeting with Rick, the City Manager, and request my attendance at the meeting also. But at this point, this issue is yours and not one that I have a high priority to pursue so I will not take the initiative to set up the meeting for you because you are mistaken about the role and responsibility the City of Alliance has (or doesn't have) with the topic you are concerned about in this discussion.

to Pasha

Don't get mad about what I said. I'm the leading preservation specialist in the region. So of course I know more about preservation work than most. I even wrote and published a book on it. And this isn't something that's putting taxpayers' money at risk. It's bringing more work to Alliance which we desperately need. It is work that should be already here in the first place. And I repeat, it's not costing the city anything. These are federal tax dollars that are supposed to be used to take care of these properties and it's not being done. There is a system that is not being used. These banks are supposed to follow those guidelines by law, and if we had people in place that knew these guidelines, it's something that could help create jobs without creating city expenses.

It's a lot different than when the city took the senior center, and the city taxi service, and KAB. That created an expense for the city and didn't create any new jobs. What I'm doing is creating more work opportunities without creating more expenses for the city. And it's work that should be done anyway.

You said you were going to do things to help contractors and this is one of those things. It's creating jobs and helping contractors and you have zero interest in this program.

Note: *Basically, getting mad because I know more about preservation than she does, where I've done it for 10 years and she hasn't done anything in the property preservation field, is really stupid to be mad about something like that. That's like going to the doctor and being pissed that the doctor knows more about medicine than you. Well, NO SHIT.*

Posha

Scott- What program are you talking about in your email? What Federal program is this that offers Federal Funds for Municipal Governments to clean up foreclosed properties?

How can I have zero interest in this program if I don't know what program you are talking about?

None of your letters to me or to the City Council actually talk about a "specific" program. Can you share a web page with me or documentation that outlines the program you are talking about? What is the name of the program?

I am interested in supporting contractors and minimizing any roadblocks any business encounters for them to do their jobs successfully. And in fact, if you weren't aware, there are actually three contractors on City Council, and I am not one of them. It is possible that supports local contractor businesses will be supported by the majority of the City Council. Please tell me how this program you are talking about will help contractors with their businesses?

Please send me a link to this Federal program so that I can read about it and educate myself.

to Pasha

http://www.safeguardproperties.com/

Safeguard properties are the national contracting companies that manage most of the HUD properties in the area. When I say HUD, I'm not talking about South Potash. I'm talking about Fanney Mae, Freddy Mac, and Greeny Mae. Our area is mostly Fanney Mae. On that site, you should be able to register as a contractor and have them send you a vendor packet which will have in detail the program they push.

The guild lines they are supposed to go by are what they write up, but also follow FHA and HUD guidelines. There are a lot of gray areas in those contracts, which I want to take to the Legislature if I can get a hold of Tom.

http://cubicyard.us/ the cubic yard site is more of a training and info site.

here is the HUD link:

https://hudgov.prod.parature.com/link/portal/57345/57355/Article/8914/What-is-the-maximum-property-preservation-allowance-and-when-must-a-mortgagee-request-over-allowable-approval

On this site, it has a block grant for code enforcement. Which I would want to be part of. Since this is my presentation.

http://cqrcengage.com/iapmo/CDBG

There used to be a state grant as well.

Posha:

Thanks for this link. I'll read through it, and I can ask Rick if we would be eligible for these types of funds, and if we are, would the program be beneficial to the City to apply for their funding program.

If you would like to share this link to the program with Rick yourself, please feel free to do so.

To Posha:

It would probably be best if you forward the info we talked about. I don't have a direct link to Rick. Everything I send goes through Jines. And I don't know how informed he is on what we've talked about. I've only talked to him one time. Just let him know that he can call me any time to go into more details. But, I do have to go do some work out of town tomorrow, but should be in town Thursday and Friday.

From my first meeting with him, he seems like he wasn't going to take anything I said seriously. Maybe he's not that way but for a first impression, that's what I got out of the meeting.

Pasha:

Okay, I will forward it to him and mention it to him. With the holiday weekend coming up, it's not likely anything will get attention until after the holiday. I will be leaving out of town on Friday and will be out of touch with anyone until after July 6.

Note: After a couple of hours of emailing messages back and forth, Pasha started to understand what I was talking about. Basically, if you want to know what's going on, you ask the professional. Many times something had been presented to the city council and they didn't understand it. Rather than getting educated about the subject, they decline it because they didn't understand it and were confused. Only a lazy fool will refuse to do something because they don't understand something. The correct thing is to get educated. If you master the system, know the system, go above and beyond your work requirement, you can bring in well over 300 grand a year into the community. That would help many contractors and laborers. When we are facing one of the highest unemployment rates and highest forecloser and bankruptcy in the history of Alliance, you don't scoff or brush off the opportunity to bring in more work and money into the area.

Message to Ryan Reynolds (City Council)

I guess Pasha is mad now because I said that I know more about the property preservation business than the city management and council. I don't know why she would be mad. Because I'm the one that does have the training and experience in that field for more than 10 years and nobody else has. And I'm the most experienced in the region. What I proposed would add more work and jobs to our area without increasing debt for the city and she doesn't support that.

I think it's more along the line that she doesn't support it because she doesn't understand it. And she doesn't support it because of probably some made-up personal issue she has against me.

6 July 2017

Scott: after emailing back and forth for a couple of hours and sending her a few links on preservation companies, training, and a link for a grant for code enforcement, she started to come around.

Ryan: right on

Scott: well, still no sit down. or any progress. Basically, the system is probably confusing and complicated for someone that hasn't done preservation work and has to deal with FHA codes. It's a snap for me because I've done it for over 10 years. Basically, Posha was going to dismiss the whole idea because she was confused by what I was presenting. To me, it didn't seem like that difficult of a task or decision.

Ryan: I think you deserve the respect of a decision, it might be yes or it might be no, but at least a decision would be made and you would know where you stand

Scott: according to Posh, if no city council member shows interest, the project pretty much dies and is forgotten.

Ryan: One could argue that an interest in something doesn't always mean that it is in favor of the topic. An interest in a specific topic could also mean a strong opposition to it.

Scott: well, what I was proposing is to change the focus of the "code enforcement officer", to something more constructive that instead of being focused on how Cox ran things by harassing people until people lost their homes or business or just got sick and tired of the harassment and decided to move. I am presenting something more useful that could create more contractor jobs. But you have to have someone in place that actually knows how to do that.

Tony is an alright person, but she doesn't know anything about city code or FHA code and how to make that benefit the city and create work. And there would not be much work that the city would have to do. It's work that a contractor can do. But you have to know what to look for and Tony just doesn't have the experience.

Posha didn't know about the budget for the code enforcement job. I know there used to be a grant award each year for that. And the job was passed around from the KAB to the building inspector than to the dog catcher. But, it took me about 5 minutes on google to find a federal grant for that.

I told her that I presented the plan so I want that position and I'll show them how to create jobs with that program.

Ryan: Okay, first of all, KAB never has and hopefully never will have the authority to act as code enforcement. Any citizen can call make a complaint about something that is a code violation. For example, an elderly neighbor of mine that lives across the street from me was frustrated with the state of the yard next to her. The house has been abandoned for some years and as a tight niche neighborhood, we all know who owns the house. She didn't know who to call or even want to be a target of harassment from the individual so I told her I would call the appropriate authorities to get the issue resolved.

I did this and then two days later the yard was taken care of by a local yard maintenance contractor. I wasn't acting as a member of KAB or the City Council. Just a good neighbor.

No big deal.

nothing less and nothing more

Scott: I think the KAB had the code enforcement job when we started using that years ago.

I have tried working with Tony and educating her and police officers on how to get these abandoned houses taken care of and they just don't do what is needed to get things done.

Ryan: Actually KAB acted as a good neighbor many years ago and got the bad rap as being the code enforcement agency.

Scott: ah, ok

Well, that one chick was kind of an asshole about things.

But, basically, as far as code enforcement there was an issue on 315 Niobrara. it's an abandoned house and had high weeds. For what we have now we would only address the high grass and weeds. For someone who knew the system, they would make a push for getting the unsecured building secured and address the garage that was leaning and about ready to fall down.

Me as an inspector, I did contact the code enforcement officer, she couldn't be reached. So I contacted the building inspector. I got the contact info for him and he called a couple of times. Which pushed the work order to fix or tear down the garage. They sent me to bid the teardown and it took 2 months for the work order to process.

Somebody else got the teardown. But with a little help from the building inspector, helped push a work order. But there should have been a push on the building not being secured. And the garage should have been tagged. If it was taped off and tagged that could have pushed that work order faster.

Another abandoned property or bank-owned property that was located on BigHorn Avenue, there was an issue that our code enforcement officer would only address the high grass. But an educated person in that field would address the gutters falling down that could fall on someone and they could address the peeling paint, which is a health hazard. That could have added another $4000[1] in work.

Ryan: Okay, you are really sending me mixed signals here because I am fairly certain that you are a registered Republican. Most Republicans I know strive for less government interference in anything.

Scott: the houses are banked owned. They have to keep these properties in FHA code. Banks usually use federal tax dollars to do this. A code enforcement officer doing just a little work could force or push these banks to create the work orders. The work orders would be done by private contractors or sub-contractors and not the government.

Ryan: Scott, you also have to realize that if win a seat on the City Council or are granted a position on the planning commission, you can't possibly vote on something like this if it came up. You must abstain from things where you could personally have financial gain.

Plus you just said it yourself....federal tax dollars. FEDERAL. completely different bodies of government.

Scott: we're not going to the federal government / HUD to change their program. Where just having a code enforcement officer being educated on the system to help push more work our way.

the banks have to abide by FHA and city code

and most of that is, what's a code violation and posting a tag on a door to fix the violation and let the inspector do the rest.

Ryan: Here is the blunt truth, you know I have a contracting business, Brian Mischnik has a contracting business, Ralph Yeager is a contractor, Pasha's husband has a contracting business. Now I can't

---

1.   https://www.facebook.com/

speak for the rest of them officially, but I am guessing that they would agree with me when I say we don't need to push any more work our way. Not only that, once again, it would be illegal for any of us, or would at least create the perception of misconduct, if we said otherwise.

Scott: the last I checked. we were #6 in unemployment in the state. We need the work.

Ryan: that statistic is probably correct.

However, I would argue that it is because the 6 percent is not very qualified.

I can't find people that can pass a drug test, have no felonies, come to work on time, do what work they claim they can....and so on and so on

I am sure that you are very good at what you do. I have never seen your work or heard anything good or bad about it.

Scott: were number 1 in unemployment in this area and the surrounding counties. that's 8 counties. and we are probably going to be #1 in foreclosures. With my inspection load, our town is the highest in 8 counties.

Well, I've had those troubles in the past with workers too. But if any contractors work on any bank-owned properties they would have to pass a background check.

Ryan: I do background checks...most fail.

If your thing is doing bank-owned properties then that's great. I don't get involved with them because it's not usually that great of quality of work and also it takes forever to get paid.

Scott: Yeah, some companies pay every 2 weeks, some 3 weeks. Some companies push the big work order payouts to 2 to 3 months. And a broker-owned house you might not get paid until the house is sold, which could take a year or so.

I'd like to see it get back to the 3-week payouts.

For the past 2 or 3 years, they have been pushing the 60 to 90 days, because after 90 days they don't have to pay you for the work because it is past the mechanical lien time frame.

Ryan: Well, either way, we all have our hang-ups. Once again, as you pursue an office in any entity, leave the personal stuff at home, you can't vote on it or bring it to the table anyway. Look at it as more of a duty to others.

Scott: well, I'm not in office and I still can't bring it to the table

so, whatever personal stuff that's at the city council, they need to put that aside, and do what's best for the city.

If I was on the council, I would still push the procedure change in the code enforcement officer position.

Ryan: Let it go then, don't bring anything of an agenda to the table. Fight and be a voice for others. To be bluntly honest, I'm not sure I agree with where you are going with the foreclosure property code enforcement. I'm giving you my time and listening though...or reading rather since it's text.

Scott: all it is, is just educating the code enforcement officer by doing a little push on these foreclosed bank-owned properties to get the work done that should be getting done. This is work that is supposed to be done anyway. But they are not creating the work orders. These contracting companies that are hired by the banks are paid to get the work done, but they are not doing it.

To get a simple grass cut done just takes a tag on the door, and then it'll end up being on a regular schedule.

on this issue, I've held the Code Enforcement Officers hand to walk her through how to do this. If she just calls the number on the door it'll take her months to get them to take care of a lawn. If you take the whole job a step further, these foreclosed properties have to meet a certain standard before the banks can sell them. Which most don't meet the standard. But, that's something different that could be pushed through legislation. The excuses I've gotten from tony and other police officers are that it is next to impossible to get these banks to take care of those properties. With what little guidance that I provided, we actually got some of the work done. If it was done exactly how I said to get it done, it would have been done a lot quicker.

Ryan: Okay, regardless of what code enforcement can or cannot exercise. You are basically saying that you are willing to place short term microeconomics for personal gain ahead of macro-economics

Scott: each foreclosed property has an inspector that checks in twice per month, and then the broker has to inspect it at least once per month. They'll do the pictures of the house, take a picture of the code infraction, and that goes to the contracting company, who puts out the work order.

Ryan: Alright, this might be a good dialog.....let me ask you a straightforward question. It's a yes or no.

Also, I will follow that question up with another yes or no question.

Is Alliance NE the only city in the Union that has foreclosed bank-owned properties?

Scott: no

Ryan: Is the State of Nebraska the only state in the Union to have foreclosed bank-owned properties?

Scott: yes

of course not

Ryan: lol, I was wondering there for a second

These are very smart companies these banks.

Scott: but, in other cities in Nebraska and other states the code enforcement officer does what I'm proposing.

Ryan: They have fantastic lawyers and have been setting precedence for a long time.

They know the ins and out as if it were a science

Scott: Yeah, but, they have to follow each state's statute and city codes. Their lawyers can't get around that if we hold them accountable. If we ignore it, they can get away with anything.

Ryan: Especially since banks NEVER want to foreclose on a property. They hate it. Too much work and money get lost.

Scott: I mean, Wellsfargo still owes me $5300[2] and Fannie Mae owes me over $8300[3] from last year.

I'm pretty sure a bank "getts wood" over foreclosures in this area

if they wanted to cut down on the foreclosures by at least half in the state, they could have passed my bill I sent threw a couple of years ago.

Ryan: What you are proposing adds a significant amount more risk to lenders and banks if a property is foreclosed on. This drives interest rates up, makes it harder for first-time home buyers, and generally causes a housing crash.

Scott: interest rates go up, depending on the percentage of allowable is given by the Federal Reserve. if they are far from their max, the interest is low, when they have a high loan total, then the rates go up.

Ryan: rates will go up depending on the exposure of risk to the lender.

Scott: most foreclosed properties, the banks, or federal reserve have already doubled their money, and they'll do it again by the sale.

Ryan: Major lenders will see too much risk, stop lending, and cause the Federal Reserve to take the appropriate action.

Lending now resumes at a level that is traditional with trends that have yielded short-term and long-term financial solvency.

Scott: with that, if you look at the paperwork that I do on inspections, our city is a high-risk city to invest in. What I get in paperwork in just alliance, is the total of what I used to get for the entire region.

Ryan: I do agree with that, but I believe that this is a cyclical phenomenon. Now is the time to buy in my opinion.

---

2.   https://www.facebook.com/

3.   https://www.facebook.com/

Scott: well, the only way to make it a city to buy into, there needs to either be more business coming to town or you create a retirement town so you got retirement money investing here.

Me, I've already lost over 200 grand in investments over the past year. So I'm pretty well spent for at least another year.

Ryan: We can't win them all. Anyway, I really have to get to sleep, got to start all over again tomorrow.

Scott: ok, catch ya later. on another note, we probably need to look at a way to expand the local HUD program

Notes: I guess, the odd thing about this discussion is, because there are contractors on the city council and they are too busy to take any more contractor work, they assume that the city doesn't need any more work. They think that since they are too busy to take on any more work than all the other contractors are too busy too. Their only focus is on themselves and their own business. There are many contractors in Alliance that could use the extra business. The city council needs to get out of its little box and start thinking of what's right for the city. A good code enforcement officer can push on abandoned and foreclosed properties and force these property management companies to do their jobs. But, a good broker could take the reins and do the same thing.

I found it odd that the city clerk claimed that this was a personal issue that needed to go to the city manager and the council member Ryan made the same claim. So they claim that it is personal so they can brush it off and not do anything.

There are some serious law violations that should be investigated. The unjust enrichment procedure is done when a contracting company forces you to sign a waiver not to lien and if you lien will charge you $50,000 for breaking their contract. That puts them in a position to not pay contracts and could be considered support of slave labor. There is also Wellsfargo's enrichment violation by charging $250 for an incorrect window tag placement for a job that usually only pays $8. Those penalties should be fairly easy to argue. But the government ignores those infractions to support the push to make banks unbreakable. Which was a prevision that started during the Bush administration due to the 2008 recession and is still being pushed today.

The conversation between the two Council members did not go all that well. I think they could not comprehend what I was trying to tell them. I was presenting them a way to add more contractor work by making sure that the banked-owned homes there were taken in foreclosures were being taken care of. Banks are supposed to hire out contractors to take care of those properties. Before those properties can sale they have to be brought up to FHA or HUD code. But they also have to abide by the city code. I think those two were still a bit confused about this type of business. But the next chapter (which is a research analysis on the conflicts between contractions and the banking industry) should have a better explanation of this type of business.

23 August 2017 (info going to the city manager and council to request to be on Agenda)

CITY COUNCIL AGENDA REQUEST FORM

Agenda Item: *Code Enforcement Officer Redefined*

Proposed Agenda Date:

Name of person(s) proposing item: *Scott Bolinger*

Contact number of person(s) proposing item: *308-762-7346*

Brief description of agenda item: *Redefining the job duties and focus of the code enforcement officer*

Discussion points:

Desired Outcome: *I'd like to see more focus on abandoned, bank owned & broken down properties. If done correctly, it could create such needed jobs.*

Approved for placement on Council Agenda: __________
City Manager

This request must be submitted to the City Clerk no later than seven (7) business days prior to the City Council meeting. Items submitted after this deadline, if complete, will be scheduled for the following City Council meeting.

Signature of person requesting agenda item   7-31-2017
Date

cc: City Manager
Assistant City Manager
City Clerk
City Attorney

Code Enforcement Officer
Redefine

When this position started about 8 or so years ago, it started as part of the KAB, then pushed to the building inspector, and then bumped to being part of the dog catcher's job. For the most part, this job has mainly consisted of getting involved in complaints about private owners' properties. In many cases, this position has been used in an unethical and harassing way, and some cases involved fraudulent paper trials. There have been issues of properties that have been taken care of on a weekly basis and despite their regular maintenance, the code enforcement officer or law enforcement officers are sent weekly anyway. Some, to the extent of people having to sell their property and move away.

This position can be used more positively. There were grants given to run this program. I don't know if the city is still using those grants. If I was in charge of this program, how I would change this to help benefit the city more positively is to seek out more grants. I've already sent grant information to the city council. The way that funds would be used is to pay my fees. If I'm sent out to inspect a property on a complaint it would cover an inspection fee. If a property owner cannot clean up a yard, if it's because of not physically able or doesn't have the money to get the property taken care of then I'd use grant funds to cover the cost of cleaning up the property. Rather than charging the property owner, I'd use the grant funds to cover costs. The cost can be discussed to establish a set base standard price.

The other part of the job is keeping track of abandoned, broker owned and bank-owned property. This has not been done very well. This is something that I've discussed with a couple of city council members, code enforcement officers, police officers, and building inspectors. I've talked to these people, told them how to get these properties maintained. Many agree to do that or think that is the way to get it done but in the end, they just don't do the work. Some properties have been sitting for over a year and haven't been touched. These properties are inspected at least twice per month, but no maintenance has been done and they are supposed to be maintained regularly. If these properties are handled correctly it could create several hundred thousand dollars in contract or subcontract work which we disparately need. Wright now, if a code enforcement officer gets called to a property they might call the number that's on the door, and they might get the yard taken care of for maybe a month or two down the road. But, what I would do as a code enforcement officer is take a walk around the building and post a code violation posting on the front door. I'd write down all violations. If it has peeling paint, tall grass or weeds, debris, unsecured building, infestation risks, trip hazards, trees in the walkway or over the street, weed control, any safety hazards.

What I've had a hard time getting across to city workers is that a simple violation tag goes a long way in getting banks and brokers to force and approve work orders. And in many cases works a lot quicker than a phone call. A phone, they'll brush you off to a different department who will brush you off to another then another one and you spend all day on the phone and you might get to the person that makes the decision. With a tag, an inspector will eventually see that and send it through. In most cases sending a picture of the code violation forces the work order.

Another program that could be set up is having a community cleanup day. KAB used to do that a few years back and it was a good program. That got many people together to volunteer to help clean up many areas of town.

When looking for grants, you would look for code enforcement officer, or Nuisance abatement programs.

http://cqrcengage.com/iapmo/CDBG

https://portal.hud.gov/hudportal/HUD?src=/program_offices/comm_planning/communitydevelopment/rulesandregs/memoranda/codeenfi95

http://www.changelabsolutions.org/sites/default/files/Up-tp-Code_Enforcement_Guide_FINAL-20150527.pdf

Analysis of the conflicts of Property Preservation and the Banking Industry.

The relation between the Property Preservations contractor and the Banking industry.

Is there corruption in the industry?

By Larry Bolinger

What is the business of Property Preservation and the working relations between contractor/sub-contractors, the banking industry, and realtors?

The business of Property Preservations and how that correlates with the banking industry starts when a mortgagor fails to make a payment on their mortgage. When that happens, the bank contracts with companies that have a network of inspection contractors. Those networks of contracting companies are also called vendors. The inspector (also called field inspector) will go to the properties to verify if the properties are occupied or abandoned. If they are found to be abandoned, the inspector will post a note for the mortgagor to contact their bank. After 2 weeks have gone by and no answer and the property still looks vacant, the bank will make an order to the vendor to send a sub-contractor to secure the building. A property is usually not acquired by the bank unless there are at least 3 months of missed mortgage payments. When the contractor goes out to secure a building they will usually change out a secondary lock, secure the property by fixing any broken windows, do a full inspection of the property and report any damages, debris, personal items, and perform a winterization and yard service. That is the extent of a home that is in presale or pre-foreclosure. In a pre-sale, the mortgagor still has rights to the property and can take it over at any time. After a legal sale of the property is completed, the bank takes full ownership and the mortgagor has no more rights to the property. The bank will then make an order request for a full post-sale work order. They will normally contact their vendor that has a network of contractors that will complete a full secure service of the property, remove and discard all debris and personal items, fix safety hazards, do a maid service and bid any other work they believe needs done to bring the property to FHA or HUD code or what is considered getting a property into compliance. The contract work could extend into roof repair, plumbing repair, mold mediation, door, and jamb replacement, fence repair, trimming trees, repair patio to full remodel to get the property in saleable condition. Any time there is an inspection or work to be done, the contractor takes a full set of interior and exterior set of photos. Then if work is done they will also take before, during, and after pictures of all work completed. All those pictures are sent to the contracting company and their quality control for review before processing. After that, the bill is sent to the bank. The contracting company normally takes 25% off the top for themselves for all contract work. After the completion of any work, the bank or vendor will send an inspector to the property to do a quality control inspection to verify the work is completed correctly. After that, they will send the contracted realtor or broker to verify that the work was completed to satisfaction. After the work is approved, then the bank pays out for the completed work. Sometimes the work is contracted from bank to realtor, to contractor. Sometimes it is Bank to the vendor with realtor management, to the contractor; sometimes it is a bank, to a vendor, to the subcontractor, to another subcontractor. Sometimes it's a vendor of a vendor that contracts with the bank. But in all cases, there is a realty broker that is contracted to the property as part of that management team.

My personal experience in the property preservation business is that I have been a contractor for over 20 years, I have subcontracted work in the property preservation field to do both inspections and property preservation work for over 13 years. I have first-hand seen the trend of the past 13 years with the change in payouts and the change in relations between contractor and vendor. I have also published a book called "Property Management by Scott Bolinger", which goes through in detail of property management and property perseverations. There seems to be a growing issue of vendors or banks not paying contractors for the work they have done. 5 years ago that did not seem to happen. But for the past 3 years, it seems like it has become the norm. My worst year, I had over $20,000 that wasn't paid out by the bank for work that I had done. After talking to many contractors and reading on property preservation in several online groups it looked like reducing pay, with holding pay, and penalizing work has been happening regularly.

Hypothesis

I hypothesis that the rate of work order rejection has increased over the past 12 years. In proving that hypothesis I would have to gather information on total work orders and total rejected work orders and review the trend over the past several years. I may have to prove certain unethical enrichment practices. I believe that there may be a trend during the time President Bush made a statement to safeguard the banking system, which then made a push for the bank bailouts for economic recovery. Many questions come up when discussing this issue. Several of the questions are as fallow: Why do banks refusal to pay contractors after work is done. Why is there a lien waiver form? If they are following FHA regulation, properties should have maintenance done regularly. But some don't until you involve the local government. Is money still being paid out to the banks with federal tax dollars even though they don't follow the FHA guidelines on taking care of bank-owned properties? Is it standard practice for a bank to cut prices on all orders? Is it standard practice to refuse to pay contractors even if the work is done, but one picture may be foggy? Why do banks force contractors to buy insurance at their preferred insurance companies rather than just listing what is needed for proper coverage? Many questions arise in the research, so I have to limit the search and focus on two areas. My primary research is to prove that rejected work orders have increased over the past 12 years. Focusing on the trends from 2005 to 2017. Some of the research will go through some enrichment practices and concerns.

From the earlier years of 2005 to roughly 2011 the pay was good and then things started getting stricter with added penalties. The banking and realty business started cutting prices, refusing to pay contractors, and creating back charges. Is it done just to enrich the banking industry? Fannie Mae, Freddy Mac, and Ginnie Mae were taken over by the government in the big bank bailout so they are owned by the Federal Government and are part of HUD. Fannie Mae is the leader in the HUD industry for foreclosed homes and creates the trends. There are several questions: Are their actions in conflict with the "enrichment act"? Is it slavery? Is a waiver of rights illegal? Why would the government approve a program that cons contractors out of work pay? So the big question would be, is it standard practice for

HUD to get out of paying contractors using a manipulated system to help feed the Federal Reserve?

Literature Review: Pre-recession research (before 2008)

Wilkins Tess, (2010), theory is that "parties were more willing to exploit a breach opportunity when a contract includes a liquidation damage clause". (Wilkinson Tess). Normally parties will act as to have interpersonal obligations unless there are uncooperative behaviors. When that happens they are more willing to exploit efficient breach opportunities. The study may help answer why a contractor would work for a bank, be denied payment, or was back charged on a work order, or the work orders were cut and continue to work for a bank out of a feeling of obligation.

I can truly understand where Wilkinson is coming from in his explanation. I had gone out of my way to do extra work in hopes to get more work. I've taken jobs and traveled a long distance with a payout that was less than the expenses to complete the job just to keep the vendor happy and to continue being on their top contractor's list to be able to get more jobs. Then the day you complain you could get a decrease in jobs or lose your contract.

According to the "Franchise Law Journal", a contractor agrees to work for a franchise and what is included is a liquidations clause in the contract, so "they are agreeing to a certain computation of potential damages before a breach of contract ever occurs. A liquidated damage amount is disproportionate when that amount is disproportionate to the actual harm. "(Franchise Law Journal).

Franchise Law Journal (2010). "In theory, liquidated damage is an unenforceable penalty when the actual damages are markedly less than the stipulated contract damages. But in practice, the courts will enforce a liquidated damages clause if it provides a reasonable forecast of the loss expected to result from a breach. "(Franchise Law Journal). With that type of policy, the contractor would not necessarily have to have done damage but would have made a possible error or infraction of the contracted policy and if the franchising agency can guess a possibility of a certain amount of damage could prove the contractor liable. What is to be considered is if the liquidated damages are exclusive under state law and this may depend on the interpretation of that clause. By interpretation could mean that you have to present a claim that could be less than the possible loss, but also could be interpreted that you would have to prove equal loss.

In Nebraska, you can enforce liquidated damages if when there are one of two factors that would occur:

1. "The damages are a reasonable estimate, determined at the times the contract was entered of damages probably caused by a breach
2. They are reasonably proportionate to the actual damages that occurred as a result of the breach. "(Franchise Law Journal).

What this study shows is that several different types of franchises including banks utilize the "liquidated damages clause." Several cases were shown that sometimes they won the case and sometimes they did not follow the guidelines and the defense won the case. So this has been used to charge contractors. That could prove or create an argument that could have shown the justifications of back charges. But as contractors, they sign a legal document to work for the franchise and abide by their liquidation clause. They are also signing away their right to lien waiver as a scare tactic to make it look like contractors can't legally fight a claim. So this does bring up questions of how legitimate the use of the liquidation act or clause is. It is a clause that could be used to protect a bank or protect the contractor.

Gottieb Richard, Rhiew Margaret, Natareli Brell, (2013). The write-up in "The Business Lawer", by Gottieb Richard, Rhiew Margaret, and Natareli Brell, talks about vacant property ordinances and how the effects foreclosures have on the communities. Cities sued banks claiming they were at fault for not taking care of those properties. They claimed it causes devaluing of property and increased crime rate. It argues who is responsible for the property and when. If a property becomes abandoned and has a default, then the bank can claim ownership as a presale. Post sale is after the bank has full ownership of the property. This creates a grey area of a semi-legal /illegal act of trespassing. Some areas created a program to fast track the foreclosure process, as well as a program that helped code enforcement officials quickly identify and correct code violations. This write-up doesn't prove any part of my theory. But it does explain the business and how contractors work to keep the vacant / foreclosed houses to code and it may give some clarity as to the type of business that banks coordinate in the property preservation field.

Sarshik Barbara, (1980's). Sarshik Barbara had written an article in "The Urban Lawyer", on recovering construction losses from HUD. This article goes through the difficulties contractors had faced when trying to get paid. HUD mortgage insurance has created some difficulties in fighting to get paid, such as having contractors waive their rights to file mechanical liens.

"The National Housing Act is the basic program or prototype of other HUD mortgage insurance program." (Sharchik). The standard process is set up by HUD and FHA. In part of the process of a contractor being paid, 10% of their funds were held to ensure that the job got done to satisfaction. Later it was changed to dispersing the funds, but an agency held the funds until they were satisfied with the completed work. That is how insurance loss, such as damages done to a house by hail damage is done. A little odd that it is being done on HUD foreclosed houses. To me, it was odd that the money was disbursed to the franchise agency, (also called nationals or vendor) but the contractors did not get paid for 45 to 90 days after a job was completed.

On the equitable theories, suits were filed because the actions of not being paid or paid being withheld were "based on equitable doctrines of unjust enrichment and quantum meruit rather than any express or implied contract. " (Sharchik pg. 297). In the case of Trans-bay Engineers and builders V. Hills, the contractor agreed to a construction contract that the loan company had defaulted on. The default notice was given to HUD. The court end result had decided that the contractor should not be made to suffer and that the mortgage company was fully insured in its loan by HUD. In another case the court ruled in favor of the contractor and that he could have a quantum meruit claim against HUD. The standard action would be to file a mechanical lien through the country clerk's office that usually costs around $10. Filing a lien has no court hearing. Unless they attempt to try and get the lien dropped through the courts rather than paying what is owed to the contractor. However, claims against HUD can be dismissed based on a defense of sovereign immunity. The reasoning for that is that a suit against HUD is a suit against the United States. Because the funds would come from the United States Treasury. That does give an odd twist to the defense of suit against HUD and how sovereignty can be interpreted. Sovereignty is usually a state, not a department unless your interpretation is that the department is the state because it is paid by with state funds. The decision on that could change depending on how the judge interprets that law. Congress would have to pass policy to define sovereignty or change how they define sovereignty or what is allowed to be considered part of a sovereign. If HUD claims to be part of the state and cannot be sued because they claim sovereignty, one could assume to defend themselves by the use of civil rights using due process and arguments against unjust penalties and slavery.

"Another theory is that claimants clause waiting to be heard against HUD do to a court decision in Aetua casualty surety company the V. United States, under the Tucker Act. The claim must be liquidated or unliquidated damages in cases not covered in tort are recognized by the constitution, state and or federal laws." (Sharshik pg. 312). Some causes failed when presented as a mechanical lien, but approved when presented as a doctrine of equitable lien and unjust enrichment, but some were denied under the Tucker Act.

What our government had done is change the characterized role of HUD from a mortgage lender to an insurer of mortgages to create a way so that HUD can claim to only be responsible to the mortgage lenders. By doing that HUD has no obligations to pay contractors.

In 2008 we were in a recession and then came along the big bank bailouts. Banks such as Fanny Mae, Freddie Mac, and Ginnie Mae were bailed out and became owned by the federal government. Which those banks in the property preservations business are called HUD and those foreclosed properties are called HUD foreclosed homes. In my opinion, it was an obviously false claim to claim to be not responsible. Basically, any bank can claim to be an insurer, because they get the actual home loan money from the Federal Reserve. But, it is not the Federal Reserve that enacts policy or approves or disapproves contract work on foreclosed properties. So there is room to argue and change the interpretation of the backing of that policy.

Sarshik did conclude that these cases prove that there is more work to be done and that the rulings were flawed. I do agree with her findings. This does help prove in a way of my theory that banks do try and get out of paying contractors in a roundabout way with the help of government policies. Government policies that give leeway so HUD can claim sovereignty to make it so they can't be sued or they change their character from a loan institute to an insurer to be able to claim not responsible may prove that the government is more at fault than the banking industry or maybe a collaboration of both entities to make the banks unbreakable.

Levine Gerald, Gordon Steven, (1990). Gerald Levine and Steven Gordon wrote in "The Urban Lawyer", theorizing "that in the next several years, the government will institute waves of civil and administrative litigation and criminal prosecution due to the multi-faceted scandals that the department of Housing and Urban Development have been part of." (Levine / Gordon, pg. 351) This goes through issues of misuse of funds and liability penalties for both HUD and contractor and with their business contracted with the lender and mortgagor. It argues that in a defaulted loan as theft, or not, or misappropriation of funds but the court rules it is not and does not fall under the theft statute. From their findings they did find that there were fraudulent actions and misuse of funds. It may prove that more stringent policies need to be created to lessen the possibility of scandals that the bank or contractor could do.

The following review of the literature has explained the many ways how our policies makers have created policies to protect both contractors and banks and in some cases are used unethically. Clauses like the liquidations damages clause to make sure claims are accurate and that liabilities had to be proven. This review goes over the process of property preservations business and how that correlates to the banking industry and the problems contractors have faced in getting paid for the work they have done. There were many safeguards done to protect banks, such as "Contract Agreements" and "Waver to Lien", agreements. Some issues of not being paid were argued under the enrichment act and quantum meuit. But to counter the possibility of HUD being sued, they claim sovereignty. What it looks like is that when the banking industry does wrong, a policy is established to safeguard them. This review goes over many of those safeguards.

Methodology

The issues in the "Property Preservation field is of interest to me and many contractors. I worked as a property preservation contractor, inspector, and quality control. There are many complaints related to these questions about the contracting companies that directly contract with HUD as well as the banks. I believe the big change in how the banking industry treated contractors and the push to get out of paying contractors started around 2012 to 2013 with major cuts in price with increased back charges and cutting agreed prices after the work was done. Then the "Waiver to Lien" came out around 2015 that started with Safeguard who directly contracts with Fannie Mae, along with forcing contractors to use their specific insurance companies, which other banks and vendors started to adopt. In some cases, insurance increased by as much a 5 times the original cost by forcing contractors to use the vendor-approved insurance companies.

I had started in the field inspection business and property preservation business in 2006. From 2007 to 2012 the payout was very good with little wait time to be paid. The pay was consistent and there were very few problems with payroll. There were never any issues or even threats of back charges or penalties for work. In 2013, problems started to emerge with banks and bank vendor's pay, which compounded more and more after each year. Looking over the foreclosure rate when the pay was good when the foreclosure rate was high and at that time, there were no problems of getting paid. One could assume the banks were making good money off of obtaining houses through foreclosures, then reselling them. Now that the rate is low, they look at ways to cut expenditures by means that could be unethical (in theory). If they were trying to budget the same way with a 2.23% foreclosure rate compared to a .51% rate and didn't adjust, could create the question of if they could have been unethical in their business practice if they did not adjust.

For the variables, there are several independent and dependent variables to consider. There are variables to consider due to a focus on the relation between the bank and contractors, but also how it correlates to the banking industry and an enrichment process. The dependent variable is the contractor's pay and the independent variable is the willingness of the banks to pay the contractor. The independent variable could also be bank policy, as well as vendor policy that can affect the contractor's pay. Another dependent variable that could concern the bank enrichment would be the mortgagor that lost their home with the independent variable as the bank policy. In a way it could be somewhat of an accretion measurement as the policies by the bank can leave a wake of destructive business practices, which can cause people to lose their homes and put contractors out of business. There can be two ways to branch the hypothesis to prove bank enrichment, but on this theory, I'm working just on the contractor and bank relation. So I will primarily focus on targeting rejected orders compared to total orders. So the independent variable would be the law and how that law could benefit HUD and the dependent variable is the denial of law. As there are laws for enrichments called the enrichment act and there are laws that cover possible property damages or possible loss of future income that can be argued under the liquidation act.

Methods

There will be several ways that I will utilize to collect the data to prove my hypothesis. I will do polls to help get a percentage of property preservation contractors that have lost income, checks being held, or cut. Then I'll do a survey to compound the poll and get a variance to be able to identify the experience of the contractor. I will review if banks are not paying the contractors and if anything has changed in the past 5 years. Then I'll have to gather information from the census bureau for total populations and then get a list of foreclosed homes total by year through the Statista. Some of my research goes back to 1980. In the '80s and '90s, there were a lot of problems with banks not paying contractors at those times too. There were many lawsuits against banks. Sometimes the contractor won and sometimes the banks won. Sometimes after a contractor won, the government creates a policy to protect the banks. That can be weighed as an unethical enrichment created by the government in support of the banking industry. The number one thing that could help my research would be if I was able to interview several processors or people who use to process work orders for banks that could give reliable answers. But that would be a low probability that someone in that position would risk giving answers to the questions that I would need to ask. So that leaves me with trying to prove an unethical enrichment practice by gathering data, running polls, doing surveys, interviews, review legal case works and government policies.

My next step in data gathering will be to research the rate of work order rejection. Compare total work orders to rejected orders, and reasons why they were rejected. There are several ways to gather that information. The first way that I would attempt to gather that information would be by contacting HUD directly and requesting that information. As HUD (Fannie Mae, Freddie Mac, and Ginnie Mae) are government-owned and controlled, that information should be readily available and attainable under the "Freedom of Information Act". A secondary way to get that information would be to talk to each contractor and get a year's work history, and a list of work rejections and reasons why they were rejected. That can be done as an interview with survey questions. The first way to obtain the research should be the quickest if they willfully follow the "Freedom of Information Act". The main areas to gather information on work orders will be from the "Property Preservation" departments of the primary banks and vendor companies. For the Banks, I would be looking at gathering information from HUD, Fannie Mae, Freddie Mac, Ginnie Mae, Wellsfargo, and U.S Bank. The vendor companies that I would focus on would be Safeguard, Five Brothers, MSI, LAS, MCS. The third area of gathering rejected and penalized work orders would be from the contractors themselves. The interview questions I would have for the banks and vendors would be:

1. In what areas were the work orders Rejected? Totals for each year 2005 – 2017
2. In what areas were the work orders penalized? Total for each year 2005 – 2017

The categories I would place these in are:

- Lack of photos or bad photos
- Late work orders
- Maid service
- Secure service
- Yard service
- Winterization
- Debris removal
- General maintenance work

The resources that I would use to gather information from banks and vendors are:

Bank Resource:

https://www.hud.gov/program_offices/housing/sfh/nsc/pandpml

https://www.hud.gov/sites/documents/16-02ML.PDF

https://www.fanniemae.com/content/tool/property-preservation-matrix.pdf

https://www.homepath.com/field-services.html

http://www.freddiemac.com/

https://www.usbank.com/splash/real-estate/bank-owned-residential-real-estate-for-sale.html

https://reo.wellsfargo.com/

Vendor Resource:

https://safeguardproperties.com/wp-content/uploads/
guidelines/FNMA/Fannie_Mae_Pricing_Rules_2013.pdf
https://safeguardproperties.com/
http://www.fivebrms.com/
http://onsitefieldserved.com/onsite-field-services.php
https://www.mcs360.com/
https://msionline.com/#/home[1]
https://www.altisource.com/Contact-Us

In collecting data through different researches I have looked at several aspects of the research to try and prove my hypothesis. I did do a poll to give a variance of property preservation contractors who have been paid, refused paid, or back charged. Then I had created a questionnaire to determine the experience or how seasoned the contractors were and how they thought the property preservations business was doing. This would help prove if the contractors were experienced and ran a profitable or successful business to help shed some light on their ability to do the job correctly and to show if they were satisfied with the way the current preservations business is going. I will then do a content analysis by reviewing online public forums that specialize in the property preservation business. With the content analysis, I will do a search of pay and review the different topics on pay to get an account of both positive and negative comments. The feedback that I'm looking for will primarily be focused on pay reliability.

In my measurements, to help prove the argument I could measure the bank's foreclosure rate before and after the 2008 recession to see if things got worse. But, I would also need to have a total populations measurement for those same times to see if the actual percentage changes and not just a direct number. Population increases so the number should increase but does it increase the total percentage? So

---

1.   https://msionline.com/#_6666cd76f96956469e7be39d750cc7d9_home

I would do both measurements from about 2005 to 2017 to create an accurate measurement

There are several ways that I would have to measure data collection. First, collect the data and then do several comparisons. My primary research is to prove the rate of work order rejection has increased or decreased. I would do a bivariate comparison to compare the rate of rejected work orders in 2005, 2010, and 2017, and compare that to the number of total work orders in those same years to see if the rates have changed or stayed consistent. This will also be multivariate with a control group. I would first measure the rate of rejected work orders for contract work on bank foreclosed homes, then compound the number of work orders on banked foreclosed homes then I'd add the control groups: property preservation, bank, vendor, Fannie Mae, Wellsfargo, US bank, Ginnie Mae, Freddy Mac. With the control groups, I'd focus on reviewing the banks as wells as the vendors that work with those banks and their property preservation departments. If the bank's and vendor's numbers don't match, then it will prove an unethical inconsistency of work orders to work order rejection.

The Secondary areas of research are to prove any inconsistencies in the housing market that could potentially lead to payouts to contractors. I would need to do a multivariate measurement of total foreclosure rate, to unemployment rate to total home loans, to show unemployment rates and foreclosure rate consistencies.

The third measurement I'd go through is a multivariate measurement showing the foreclosure rate in 2005, 2010, and 2017, which I have gathered and compared that to the measure of the total allowable money from the federal reserve for home loans, and measure that months allowable for property preservation rehab. This will show if there is a consistency of allowable funds.

Results

In a poll that was done in 2019, I have shown that there is a high rate of pay refusals and even chargebacks. I had done a poll on a property preservation site to get a number count of how many people were paid, not paid, or even received a chargeback and this is the result:

Poll Questions Totals

I have been a victim of back charges and pay refusal	60
I have been a victim of pay refusal	27
I have been a victim of back charges	13
No problems	3

The poll showed roughly 97% of the contractors had received some sort of penalty. They received a back charge, pay refusal, or a combination of both. With that poll, I wasn't able to determine if these contractors were fairly new or seasoned contractors and if there have been changes to the industry. I created a survey to help determine what percentage are seasoned contractors and how satisfied they are with the property preservations business. What the survey shows is that the majority of contractors are seasoned contractors in a multi-discipline specialty. Roughly 80% of these contractors are saying that the business is worse than it was compared to 5 years ago and that even seasoned contractors have been refused pay. The reason for no pay lacks good reasoning. 95% of those contractors have over 10 years of experience. That is a lot of seasoned contractors to have such a high amount of penalties.

Another research tactic completed in 2019 was done as a questionnaire. This was done to try and get the range of the contractor. To see how much experience they have in the field and to get their view of what direction the business has gone. This research shows that the business over the past 5 years has gotten worse and that the results of getting paid are a big factor. Most fear that they will not get paid or fear that they would have a penalty for the job they do. This also shows that a high percentage of the contractors are seasoned contractors that have had a long prosperous contracting business.

Questionnaires

Question	Choices	Result
What is your primary discipline?	• Carpentry • Mason • Locksmith • Plumber • Multi-discipline	80% are multi-discipline and 20% are carpenters
What age group?	• 18 to 25 • 26 to 35 • 36 to 55 • Older than 55	80% are between the age of 36 and 55 and 20% are in the age group of 26 to 35
How many years have you been in the property preservation business?	• Less than 1 year • 1 to 10 years • 11 to 20 years • More than 20 years	80% have been in the business between 11 to 20 years, 15% from 1 to 10 years, and only 5% that had less than one year.
Do you perform both preservation work and inspections?	Yes or No	80% said yes
Do you do both property	Yes or No	100% said yes

preservation work and private contract work?

How many work orders do you complete each month?

- 1 to 10
- 11 to 30
- 31 to 50
- More than 50

70% said more than 50, 20% said 11 to 30, and 10% said 1 to 10.

What is your average yearly income?

- Less than $20,000
- $20,001 to $50,000
- $50,001 to $100,000
- $100,001 to $200,000
- More than $200,000

1. The average is equal in each yearly income.

What is the bank that provided most of the work orders?

US bank, Safeguard, Fannie Mae, Wellsfargo.

Have you ever been denied pay?

yes or no

80% said yes

The next few questions are in reference to comparing how you feel the business is going today as it was 5 years ago	Answer with (Better, Worse, or The Same)
How do you think the preservation market is going?	80% said worse
Preservation job security is _____.	70% said worse, 20% said the same and 10% said better
The security of being paid is _____.	60% said worse and 40% said the same
The rate of pay compared to 5 years ago is_____.	60^ said worse and 40% said the same

I have evaluated contractors' negative feedback to positive feedback and their outlook towards vendors. Vendors are contracted by the banks to manage the bank owned properties. The feedbacks will primarily be focused on pay reliability. The vendor's reliability to pay is the independent variable and the contractor's feedback is the dependent variable.

My unit of analysis and units of observations will be online in a Facebook group that is made up of property preservation contractors that work with bank vendors regularly. How I will gather my information is by the group's word search to compile a quick list of responses. I would use the word search for pay, back charges, Safeguard, Fivebrothers, MSN, Wellsfargo. For each of those words, searches may give me similar or different lists. One might ask how reliable Fivebrothers pay is, and you might get several answers of positive or negative feedback.

Negative feedback _40_____

____

Positive feedback __9___

I had done a search just on "pay". I found that there were 40 negative feedbacks towards pay, reduced pay, back charges, or just not getting paid, or late payments. There were only 9 positive feedbacks where they said there were no problems. So, from those numbers that would be about an 80% negative reliability towards pay.

DATA

In my research, I have looked at different measurements to help prove the argument of the enrichment principle. I looked at measuring the bank's foreclosure rate before and after the 2008 recession to see if things got worse. But, I also looked at total populations measurement for those same time to see if the actual percentage changes and not just a direct number. The measurements that I did do were from about 2005 to 2017. The factfinder shows that the population in 2005 was 288,378,137. For 2017 the population was 325,719,178. There is some information on the foreclosure rate on Statista. It shows that the foreclosure rate in 2005 was at .46%. It was at its highest point in 2010, at a rate of 2.23%. Which was right after the 2008 recession. For the 2017 rate, that was reduced down to .51%. So comparing 2005 to 2017, there would be very little difference in enrichment. The peak years were from 2008 to 2010 which was on an incline.

Ben Carson was sworn in as the 17th Secretary of the U.S. Department of Housing and Urban Development in March 2017. Was tasked to decrease the budget for HUD. He stated that one way to cut spending is to invest in manufactured housing and push for people to buy more manufactured homes as well as modular homes and tiny homes to help tackle our growing homeless problem.

After the 2008 recession, Congress created a program called the Troubled Asset Relief Program (TARP) when Congress lent over 336 Billion of taxpayers' money to banks. Part of that agreement was to have the banks participate in a Home Affordable Modifications

Program (HAMP). That program was supposed to help homeowners gain relief and decrease the foreclosure rate. However, Wellsfargo had a glitch in their system and their numbers didn't calculate correctly, so a lot of people lost their homes that should not have. (Alystock, Witkin, Kreis & Overholtz, PLLC)So a suit was created against Wellsfargo for that infraction. In 2010 was a high point in the foreclosure market at 2.23 % foreclosure rate. Wellsfargo was in another lawsuit when they created a fake account scandal in 2016 when they created millions of deposits and credit cards to boost the sales figure. (McCoy 2016)

Conclusion

Through these 5 studies that I discussed in the "Literature Review", there are many issues that come up as ways that policy can protect the banking industry, or HUD, and or the contractors. The Federal Reserve is federal government-owned. The bank borrows money from the federal reserve for housing loans. HUD, which consists of Fanny Mae, Freddie Mac, and Ginnie Mae are banking institutes owned by the federal government. My conclusion is that our policies makers did in fact create several policies with the primary focus being to protect the banking industry. This makes it hard when a franchise that works for the bank defaults on paying contractors to be able to fight back and get paid. However, there are some policies that contractors can use to try and force payment. Banks have and will continue to try and get out of paying contractors depending on the situation. With the attempt of getting out of all pay rather than abiding by liquidations of damages clause. Because most banks will assume contractors won't fight not being paid or fight against receiving pay cuts.

In my research, I have shown that there are some unethical enrichment procedures that have been done for a long time. It shows that unethical enrichment practices have been going strong since the 1980s. I have not shown that the practices are worse now compared to then, but I have shown that it still is standard practice. I have shown that the trend of foreclosure rates by percentage is close to the same comparing 2005 and 2017, with the peak in 2010, which is before and after the recession. But, if you go by the actual numbers with 2017 having over 70 million more populations, could show that the foreclosure rate is significantly higher. But, if you compare by percentages then it would only show a .03 % difference.

There are questionable consistencies. When in 2010, the data shows that the foreclosure rate was at its highest, but contractor pay was very good, with little to no problems getting paid. So when the foreclosure rate is at its highest, that means fewer people are paying their mortgage so less money is going back to the Federal Reserve. While in 2017 the foreclosure rate is down, trying to get paid is difficult and sometimes penalized. If the foreclosure rate is down, that should mean that more people are paying their mortgage, so there should be more money filtering to the Federal Reserve. So contractor payouts should be up, not down.

My plans for sharing my findings:

There are several ways that I want to share my findings. If UNO wants to use the findings as part of a study, I would be open to that. I would have the research available for PDF or Word Doc download or print. I am also writing a book on "Business and Politics". Which will cover my time running for city council, legislature, and congress, the business I ran and how politics sometimes play into personal business, and the effects of that. I intend to also push the research to both the state legislatures and congress to review my findings and change policies. I have presented policy change requests before, but nothing has been done on housing, contractor, or foreclosure policies or how the banking industry treats contractors. I will most likely use part of my findings to help promote my campaign for congress and utilize a news outlet to help push for a review by the legislature. I would also encourage the local city council to push policy change by utilizing the "League of Municipalities" to help put pressure on the legislature. I would also seek some support from a PAC that specializes in contractor work or unions as well as a housing PAC to help lobby for changes in the industry. I would also like the IRB to review to approve further research.

Budget

What I would request is $50,000 for a 6 month to a year to research the hypothesis to prove the rate of rejected work orders and total work order consistencies or inconsistencies and if they have increased or decreased and compare those to several banks and HUD as well as vendors. I would run more polls and surveys with contractors and subcontractors and run questionnaires with representatives that are vendors and banks in the property preservation departments. The questionnaires may be done over the phone, by email, and in person. Gaining data from HUD willfully could save a lot of time in my research to prove the rate of work order rejection. If they deny the "Freedom of Information Act," then that could get costly if I was to file a formal complaint and take legal actions against the HUD department or its banking entities.

The information that I have now has created a reason to question ethical standards that needs more research. To prove both the worker order rejection rate and unethical enrichment practices the total research could take 1 to 2 years with an expenditure that could run in up words of $200,000 to be able to get direct, tangible evidence to prove my hypothesis and possibly force policy and/or procedural changes. At some stage, I may have to lobby to gain legislative support, the cost to lobby and to push research by getting congressional support could cost significant. When the research is near completion and ready to push for a policy and procedure change, I would have to lobby for congressional support. To gain information on unethical enrichment practices I would have to collect data from subcontractors, review work orders and photos of work to show if work orders were done correctly and in full, and compile 1000 rejected and penalized work orders. I would have to review any lawsuits between contractors and banks concerning non-payment for work completed as well as review mechanical liens for non-payment of work.

References

https://factfinder.census.gov/faces/tableservices/jsf/pages/productview.xhtml?src=bkmk

https://www.statista.com/statistics/798766/foreclosure-rate-usa/

wikipedia

https://en.wikipedia.org/wiki/Penal_damages?fbclid=IwAR19Np2QgVNzBNPpDUwuguXGJV8ZSseB-DiPc7U

Gottieb Richard, Rhiew Margaret, Natareli Brell, (2013), "Reckless Abandon: Vacant Property Ordinances, Create Legal uncertainties", (February), (Vol. 68 No 2) pg. 669 - 676

https://www.jstor.org/stable/23526786?Search=yes&resultItemClick=true&searchText=property&sear

Sarshik Barbara, (1980's), "Urban Lawyer", Vol 15, No. 1, pg. 291-315

https://www.jstor.org/stable/27893171?Search=yes&resultItemClick=true&searchText=recover&searc

Levine Gerald, Gordon Steven, (1990), "The Urban Lawyer", Vol 22, NO. 3, pg. 351 – 368,

https://www.jstor.org/stable/27894668?Search=yes&resultItemClick=true&searchText=recover&searc

Franchise Law Journal (2010), "Liquidated Damages", Vol.29, No 4, pg. 211-230

https://www.jstor.org/stable/
29542285?read-now=1&refreqid=excelsior%3A27f3deec8337c9fec24dc897(

Wilkins Tess, (2010), "Do Liquidated Damages Encourage Breach? A psychological experiment", (March 2010), Vol. 108, N.5 pg. 633-7-671

https://www.jstor.org/stable/
40645918?Search=yes&resultItemClick=true&searchText=liquidated&searcl

https://factfinder.census.gov/faces/tableservices/jsf/pages/
productview.xhtml?src=bkmk

https://www.awkolaw.com/
wells-fargo/?gclid=CjwKCAiAzanuBRAZEiwA5yf4usDBCPUHTB42F49p

https://dsnews.com/daily-dose/07-24-2019/revising-regulation-
to-tackle-housing-affordability

https://factfinder.census.gov/faces/tableservices/jsf/pages/
productview.xhtml?src=bkmk

https://www.statista.com/statistics/798766/foreclosure-rate-usa/

McCoy Keven (February 2016), "Fed limits Wallsfargo's growth, citing consumer abuse". https://www.usatoday.com/story/money/
2018/02/02/fed-limits-wells-fargos-growth-citing-consumer-abuses/
302973002/?fbclid=IwAR09lhrpYETq0_P5LqAwDnD5WpJ1U4QE5fMJK

AVVO (Oct. 2014), ""Can I sue a property preservation company for nonpayment?"

https://www.avvo.com/legal-answers/can-i-sue-a-property-
preservation-company-for-non—1921840.html

Bolinger Scott (2018), "Property Preservation by Scott Bolinger",
4th		edition,		http://bolinger-and-associates.com/
property-management-book.html

Bank References:
https://www.hud.gov/program_offices/housing/sfh/nsc/
pandpml

https://www.hud.gov/sites/documents/16-02ML.PDF

https://www.fanniemae.com/content/tool/property-preservation-matrix.pdf

https://www.homepath.com/field-services.html

http://www.freddiemac.com/

https://www.usbank.com/splash/real-estate/bank-owned-residential-real-estate-for-sale.html

https://reo.wellsfargo.com/

Vendor References:

https://safeguardproperties.com/wp-content/uploads/guidelines/FNMA/Fannie_Mae_Pricing_Rules_2013.pdf

https://safeguardproperties.com/

http://www.fivebrms.com/

http://onsitefieldserved.com/onsite-field-services.php

https://www.mcs360.com/

https://msionline.com/#/home[2]

https://www.altisource.com/Contact-Us

Mechanical Liens

Mechanical Liens

A mechanical lien is when a contractor puts a lien on a property after the owner refused to pay for contractor work that was done on their property. I've had to do this a couple of times with a soso response. One lien I had to file against a bank-owned property and I eventually got paid for the work I had done. But I lost the contract for that company from filing the lien. I had to sign an agreement not to work for that company ever again. That was a company that I had contracted with for about 10 years. The other mechanical lien that I had filed, the owner lost the property in a foreclosure. Banks don't pay on liens after a foreclosure. I'll explain in more detail on these two issues. One of the main issues on mechanical liens is, in most states, you have 3 months from the time of completion to file the lien. Unless you left tools and supplies there. That can stretch out the lien until you are able to get the tools and supplies.

On the first lien, it was with a company called SafeGuard properties LLC. They are a contracting company that works with Fanny Mae on foreclosed houses. This company takes care of all the foreclosed houses. They are the contracting company that hires contractors and inspectors to take care of bank-owned properties. Contractors would go to these houses, clean out all the debris, take care of the yard, do maid services on the houses, do general repairs and bring the house up to FHA code. I had been working with this company for a couple of years and never had a problem with getting the work done, getting the work order processed, and getting paid. But In any of these types of businesses, when they start switching the regional coordinator around you are pretty much screwed. Usually, they are the hatchet man. Sometimes they are replacing someone who knows the business with some pencil pusher that would need to read the directions on how to use a hammer. But, anyway. I had a clean-out in a town that was 240 miles away. I had done some work in that area before and found some people that wanted to start in the property preservation business. So I hired them to do this work. So happens that they lived next door to the property that needed work done. They had removed all the debris and did the maid service on the property and did a yard service. The job was completed and it was done correctly. They did a very nice job. But the Safeguard website had a glitch and would only accept half the pictures. So the new regional coordinator had me email the pictures. Every 2 or 3 weeks, I'd get a message saying that they didn't get enough pictures and to resend, so I'd resend everything. I had sent the pictures, which was about 400 pictures threw email roughly 15 times. Then I get a message back saying that they are not going to pay for that work order and that they will be sending another crew to do the job and that I will be responsible for the job not being done. The job was completed, and they were going to send another crew, to pretend to do the job and pay that other crew for the job my crew did. So we ended up getting the safeguard mediator to try and mediate, but the safeguard mediator's only interest was to prove that I was wrong and Safeguard was right. So I ended up filing a mechanical lien on the property. 2 or 3 months down the road, they were transferring ownership to another bank and had to pay out the lien before they could close. The cost of filing a lien is usually around $10 at the county clerks. But because I had filed a mechanical lien, Safeguard made me sign a paper saying that I agree not to work for them ever again. Basically, I was able to collect the $750 on that work order. But lost the contract that was paying me about $25,000 per year.

That is where the banks have the contractors by the balls. You can brush off the $750 and pay your contractors out of your own pocket and just eat it. If you do that you can continue to work and they might do that again. The research analysis shows that it is a norm. If you fight to get paid, you risk your contract which could cost you more in the long wrong.

The second time I did a mechanical lien was kind of an odd deal. I was running an 8 unit apartment complex. And next door to that was a 3 unit home. The owner (Cad Wait) was having some rental and sales problems with that house for a year or so. He was also having some financial problems. So he went and did a contract with a guy to sell the house for $45,000. But after several months the guy never made any down payments and then he let the property sit without heat during the winter, so all the pipes and fixtures froze and broke. He went 7 or 8 months without receiving any payments. The property looked abandoned but it did have some homeless people living in the basement. The guy that was supposed to be buying the house, started selling everything in it. He was posting stuff online selling the refrigerator and doors. So I called up Cad and was told him that I would pay $50 for that door. And he was wondering what the hell I was talking about. So I told him that the guy he was selling the house to was selling parts out of his house and I told him if he isn't supposed to be doing that he better get down here. So I told him that I'm a contractor and that I could go over and change the locks and secure the property. So I did that. And he hired me to take care of the yard for a couple of months. And one time I drove by and saw papers in the window. They were standard bank notification papers. Those are posted when someone is about to lose their house in foreclosure. So I told cad and he explained his situation. He had a bad deal in Denver that fell apart and he was trying to get his rental property issues settled in Alliance. At this time, he had this 3 unit apartment vacant for 3 years and he had another house that was a duplex that was half gutted and pipes broke. That second building looked like it should have been bulldozed over. So I told him that on the 3 unit complex that I could fix the plumbing, do some painting, get the heaters going, replace the linoleum, and repair the bathrooms to get that backup and running so it is making some rent money. So I did a full remodeling on the single room apartment on my dime. I even had to replace the water heater with an updated tankless water heater. We agreed that the rental collected would be used to pay off the contractor debt. That worked out for 2 or 3 months. Then he had a friend of his move into the 2 unit apartment for free and said he was going to do some maintenance. And then the renter on the other apartment moved out and Cad had moved in his brother-in-law into that apartment for free. And we discussed how I was going to get paid if he wasn't going to allow rental payments. And he was going to do monthly payments. Which he never did. Then he started calling and yelling at me for not paying him rent and why he wasn't getting rent. He put in his friends and relatives in the house for free and I guess he expected me to do the work and pay their way. And his renters racked up a $500 electric bill in my name. One time I had to do a plumbing job on another house, so I went to this property to get my tools. And Cad heard I went and got my tools and he got pissed off that I got my tools. So he said I was not to go onto the property again. I asked if I could get my tools and supplies. He said yes and then changed his mind several times. Then made up a bunch of excuses as to why he wasn't going to pay for the work that was done. He said his friend was going to do the work on the other apartment and get that running. So eventually, I had to file this mechanical lien.

A year later, Cad tried filing papers to get the lien lifted. So I had to re-file papers to keep the lien going. Basically, if you have something special going on with the property such as selling it or you have some grave hardship because of the lien then the courts may consider dropping the lien. It would have been dropped if I had not re-filed the papers. I found out that this guy has done this several times. In his deal in Denver, he had a partner on a multi-million dollar project that he screwed over. And there was an issue of a different contractor doing some work on another one of his properties in Alliance who he owed $1500 but he refused to pay and then he made off with the guy's trailer. Cad did not pay the contractor and then made off with his trailer. He owed me $5400 and then he made off with $600 in tools and supplies. A few years later the property I worked on was in the system and was in pre-foreclosure. I was out doing housing inspections and this house came up for an interior/exterior inspection. When Cad took over the house, he never made a dime because he let his friends live there for free. And then he caught his brother-in-law sleeping with his wife. He and his brother-in-law were seen in the backyard fighting. I didn't think too much into that, but did that mean his brother-in-law and his brother-in-law's sister was sleeping together? Gross.

In that house, Cad said that he was having a friend stay in the second unit for free but he was going to do some work on it. When I inspected the second unit it wasn't even touched. The work I did still looked fair being 5 years old. A lot of my tools and supplies were still in the basement. Wellsfargo was the bank that took control of the house. So I did get in contact with them and was about to do some work on it and get paid. But the property still had the $5300 lien on it and I had contacted them to try and get them to pay the debt. They eventually put it up for public auction. And they said that if it sells, that the bank gets paid first, and if there was anything left over I would get that. I figured the lawyer was probably full of shit and he was. I did not see a dime. The bank wasn't going to pay out anything on the property. If a private owner sold the house to a private buyer then the lien would have to be paid. But if a bank takes it over they are allowed not to be reliable to repay any debt on the property.

Risks in Property Inspections

Sometimes in the property inspections business, there are risks. You just don't know when you go out to a place that you might end up running into a nut case.

On 24 August 2017, I was having a good day until the last inspections. I did what is called a "drive-by inspection" that was 40 miles out in the middle of the country. I had seen that there were contractors at the property working. So on my way back to town a couple of them were following me and they pulled me over wondering if I was lost. I said, "No, I'm just an inspector doing some inspections." So we left it at that. Then we got another 10 or so miles down the road and this jackass was following me again and pulled us over and surrounded my car and was taking a video. I told him he needed to leave us alone that it's against the state law to stock people. One of their guys kept walking around the car and they didn't leave until another car was coming up the road. I ended up calling the police to report this. It was a pickup with no license pulling a trailer with no license. So they sent the state patrol and sheriff out to look for this vehicle. When I got home I got a hold of the broker that was contracted on that property to see who the hell that contractor was that was working on that property. And she knew nothing about any contractors. The property was supposed to close that following Friday and these contractors have been reported to have been out there for at least a month. The broker said nobody was supposed to be out there. So I ended up calling back the state patrol and letting them know. The broker said she was going to go out there in the morning. But I told her, she needed to take the sheriff or state patrol with her. Those guys were a little squirrely and not in a funny way.

I remember talking to the contractors that were there a month ago and I think they said they were out of Wisconsin. They said they were hired by the bank or person buying the property. Which, if they were hired by the bank the broker would have known and she would have been checking up on them regularly. If they were hired by the person buying the property they would not have any legal authority to step onto the property until after the closing. Those contractors being there would be considered trespassing and work done could be considered willful damage to the property. The jerks took out their phone and started recording me, so I took out mine and took a bunch of pictures of them and their car. And I told the broker that I would be interested in going with her to the property tomorrow to identify these two.

In the line of things as far as contracting goes, a banked owned property would have a broker as a managing company, and either the broker contracts directly with a contractor to do work or the bank has a nationally known contracting agency which is still monitored by the broker. So the only type of contractor that would be allowed to work on the property is a property preservation specialist that would be hired by the broker or the national contracting company. Which it looks like these guys were not.

Anyway, these two clowns thought they were being tough. They did not know who they were pulling over. They were just being dumbasses. People do have the right to conduct citizen's arrest, but they better be right about the law violations or they can be changed for the false arrest. I was the only authorized person allowed on that property. They must not have known that. They also didn't know I had 30 years of kickboxing experience and that I was also carrying a sidearm, a tazer, and pepper spray. So they put themselves in a very bad position. When people do something stupid like that, they don't think of any consequences. They really didn't know who they were chasing down and they were lucky that I was tolerant, patient and knew the laws, and knew my business. After they found out I called the State Police they took off and I went fishing.

I was contracted to over 20 National companies to conduct property or vehicle inspections. I remember one particular inspection that I received from Guardian Asset Management. They wanted me to go to a property that was on the reservation, sneak around and take 14 pictures and then sneak away. This was an inspection that I was familiar with from a company that I had done business with in the past and on their contract you don't sneak. Any agency that requests you to sneak around should be red-flagged. On the inspection itself, called for knocking on the door and then doing an interview. The homeowner was a little upset which is understandable. People who fall back on their house payments are a little stressed. But there were about 10 people that came outside to greet me. The inspection was to let them know to call their bank and if they wanted me to relay any information that I could do that and also get an updated phone number. So, I did what was required but the inspection manager for GAM got pissed that I didn't sneak around. I just told him tough shit, I didn't want to get shot. It was a Vanderbilt inspection and that I was familiar with Vanderbilt and its policy and procedures. He wanted me to trespass on the property and conduct an inspection in an unethical way. I ended up dropping that contract. It wasn't worth putting me in a bad position.

Another work order I had was to secure a mobile home. It was obviously abandoned so we got approval to secure the property and winterize it. To secure a property means that you change out a secondary lock. I had hired someone to help me out and get this property secured. The people that owned that property moved next door. The mortgagor came out and went after my hired hand and threaten that he was going to go get his shotgun if we did not leave. On that particular job, I had to call law enforcement to get things calmed down. My hired hand wasn't too excited about doing any more preservation work after that.

I've had law enforcement call on me because I was working on an abandoned property. That is the correct way on how to deal with a suspicious issue. The number one thing you should always have is the proper paperwork that allows you on the property. I never did work without it.

Tax Foreclosure Reform:
Tax Lien Reform Proposal
By
Larry Bolinger

I have dealt with quite a few tax Lien, lien foreclosures, and foreclosures over the past few years and have dealt with asset companies that were investing in a property tax lien in a gray area way. This type of business has been an aggressively growing business. Where if you're late on paying your property taxes, a company can come in, pay your taxes on your property and charge you interests. Which may be a double interest. Interest coming from the county and interest coming from the asset company. On this, if they pay 3 years of taxes, they can foreclose on your property and sell it. In this gray area of business, I know of one company that's doing this, and what they'll do is go through the courts, get their legal papers, then instead of filing the paperwork properly they pocket the paperwork, instead of having this information available at the county treasures office. So you can buy a property, check with an assessor's office and county treasures office and it will show that there are no liens and no back taxes, you do the deed transfer and it shows that you're the only owner on that deed. meanwhile, an asset company may be online trying to sell your property.

I've talked to one of these companies called US Asset that is managed by Deanna Waloca and Angela Eyrich and they are running the tax lien business "US Asset" in this manner. Pocketing the legal paperwork rather than filing them with the county treasure is an unethical business practice. Deanna says, she can hold those papers for 10 years and has the right to sell your property. The land owner can sell their property, but in that sale, they would have to pay the lien she has filed even though there is nothing on file at the court house. But she says that if she sells your property, you get nothing. I can see some of this as being a city bail-out. Where if a lot of people in the city were not paying taxes on their property and an asset company comes in and buys out a lot of taxes. But there has to be some sort of structure. It can't be set as a free for all to take people's property. There has to be structure, there has to be proper filing, land owners have to be notified beforehand, and if there is a procedure missed, then the suit is dropped. In this process, you can be late, (a day, week, month) doesn't matter how late, and an asset company can come in and make your payment and bill you an extra $500 per half. Standard is 14% but it's getting billed out at $500, which doubles some people's taxes. I'd imagine the basic theory behind doubling your taxes is to make it so high that you can't catch up, that way you are guaranteed to lose your property. I know a company that paid $6000 for the taxes and wanted $50,000 in return.

I've been buying and selling property and investing in properties for several years, and the standard is, before you buy, you check the county assessors, then the county treasure to check for back taxes and liens. I have a property that has gone through this process, I checked it, no liens, just a couple of years of back taxes, bought the property, then 7 or so months later, I'm seeing an asset company trying to sell my property. Which was this US Asset and Deanna Waloca. And when confronted about this, she said it was foreclosed, but there were no documents filed with the county treasures office, and she says that it's not her fault that I didn't hire someone to check all the legal stuff with the building before buying it. Which, the only thing I should have to do is check with the assessors and treasures office to obtain any information, about the building. I shouldn't have to hire a special investigator to dig up hidden information about the building.

Comparing our tax lien program to other states, it seems like the Nebraska tax lien program may have been implemented under some desperation without any thought of the implications put on land owners. Looks like it was created to make a quick buck for the county and a couple of asset companies. And in some cases, it doesn't make anymore because a building may have to sit and be tied up in courts for months or years and during that time it may receive multiple liens, which would make the property a very tough sale. If we continue with this, it'll eventually destroy the economy.

Proposed change:

What I'd like to see done is to go back to the system that a company cannot buy your taxes unless it's 4 years past due. Some states have it at 5 years, and will give you a year to catch up on the taxes before finalizing a foreclosure. At the moment, if you're a day past due, then people are buying your taxes and tack on a hefty penalty.

On lien foreclosures, I'd like to see this being handled with more broker involvement. If a

property is at a point that a property owner has to sell, or it is going into foreclosure, that you would be able to do a contract with a realty broker. If a person contracts with a broker, that gives them rights to manage that property and get it sold. Properties would have to meet FHA standards and be taken care of regularly, with monthly inspections by qualified inspectors.

What we have now, is a couple of companies in the state are specialized in buying property taxes to put liens on property to, supposedly stimulate the economy. That's the craziness of our government that thinks stealing people's lands helps stimulate the economy. But working things this way, only one or two are making a large amount of money off of other people's misfortunes. Basically, the poor get poorer, and the rich take advantage of the poor. So, we can have a program to get the 1 or 2 companies rich or set up a program that will help thousands live comfortably. In both cases, the taxes do get paid. And if you sign on directly with a broker, the property can be marketed quickly, rather than sitting in the loop for a couple of years in that limbo stage where nobody knows who has the rights to the property, and there's a continued legal issue surrounding the property. If a property owner signs with a broker, then that secures that property for sale. And the next thing is to make sure the property meets FHA standards for property preservation. Which standard foreclosures must meet the FHA code, while lien foreclosure there is no structure. Most brokers have a list of Property Preservation specialists in each state, and there are national registries.

To recap on this:

- We change how a tax lien company can buy people's taxes. At the moment a homeowner could be one day late and someone can buy the taxes and tack on a large fee. The change I would do is set the time frame at 4 years before a company can buy someone's
taxes.
- After the 4 years have passed the landowner would have 1 year to pay off the lien or it could go into foreclosure for the lien.
- To stop a property from going to foreclosure a landowner could contract with a Broker to sell the property and upon the sale, the lien and interest not exceeding 14% are paid to the investment company, the landowner gets paid if the property is sold for more than what he or she owes, and the broker gets his/her commission. As long as the landowner is contracted with a broker, the property can't finalize and go into foreclosure. If the property is not occupied, then the Broker will have to make sure the property is up to FHA code and being maintained. The Broker would have a choice to hire a Property Preservation specialist to

bring the building up to FHA code and do reoccurring services or have the property preservation specialist do an inspection and fill out a form to show what needs to be done to bring a property up to FHA code and the landowner would have to do the work. Inspections on the property would be paid out within 6 weeks, payouts on Property Preservation service would be upon sale of the property.

Other Items to Consider:

◈ Extending the Mechanical Lien times to 10 years. A tax lien is 10 years, might as well expand a mechanical lien to 10 years and keep it the same. Only having it at 2 years, makes it easy for people to not pay contractors.

◈ When a bank forecloses on a property, they should have to pay off any Liens just like anyone else that buys a property. If someone's sales property, and has a Lien and the lien isn't settled at the time of the sale, it could be considered fraud. But a bank is given a free pass on this fraud.

◈ During a foreclosure: it should be unlawful for a bank to publicly announce the foreclosure and time of public auction. If the bank is taking a property, they should have to assume the loan. If the property is for sale by the mortgagor, and the bank has it in pre-foreclosure and the bank is putting up ads in the paper for the public auction, that undermines the mortgagor's sales. Interested investors have turned away because of that so that they can try and pick up the property cheap at the public auction.

Books by Scott Bolinger

Bolinger Kickboxing
    2016 release, revised in 2018

Bolinger Kickboxing by Scott Bolinger (kickboxing master with over 30 years experience in martial arts)

This is an instruction manual for the Bolinger Kickboxing system. This has 394 pages and over 1000 pictures. This book goes through many aspects of martial arts: Business building and fundraising, stretching, stances, punches, and strikes, kicking, combinations, blocks, bridging the gap, exercise routines, how to make your own equipment, weight lifting, the 4 levels of boxing, medicine ball routines, speed drills, heavy bag drills, a self-defense course, rules and regulations for several combat sports, how to wrap your hands.

Hard cover: Item# 1000 $75.00

CD: Item# 1000CD $45.00

Ebook: Item# 1000EB $40.00

Boxing Basics by Scott Bolinger Level 1 of 4

This book goes through the level one medicine ball routine and level one coaches mitts routine and boxing work out. It also goes through a beginner's heavy back routine and shows the different strikes. The level on boxing routine sets the base set of combinations, that's your bread and butter combos, in the second round combinations that are to help more with hand-eye coordination with working 2 combos at the same time as well as working how to jamb, counter and get off the ropes. The Level 1 medicine ball routine is a very good starter exercise to help tone and has been used to rehab shoulders.

Ebook item # WR1E $7.99

Paper Back Item # WRIP: $12.99

pack of 10 Item WRIP10: $100

Boxing Basic by Scott Bolinger Level 2

This book goes through the level 2 medicine ball routine and the level 2 boxing mitt routine. In the level 2 mitt routine, you start working on some basic defense. In the Bolinger boxing program, we don't just teach blocking as a single act, we teach block and counter. There is also a chapter that has a more advanced heavy bag routine.

The medicine ball routine levels 2 and 3 are advanced routines, you should be in fair shape when starting on those, but good for full-body workouts. The level 2 mitt works start you out in the full set of defensive combos as well as defense and counters.

Ebook item # WR2E $7.99

Paper Back Item # WR2P: $12.49

pack of 10 Item WR2P10: $100

Boxing Basic by Scott Bolinger Level 3 & 4

This book shows the level 3 and 4 medicine ball routine and the level 3 and 4 coaches mitt routine. Level 3 medicine ball is an advanced exercise routine, level 4 you'll need a partner for that exercise routine. Level 3 mitt work is more advanced block and counter. In level 4 mitt work, you're working the jab, pressuring, and working striking angles.

Ebook: Item# WR3E $7.99

Paper Back: Ityem# WR3P: $12.49

Pack of 10: Item# WR3P10: $100

National Self-Defense Solutions

This book outlines a step-by-step seminar for a self-defense and restraint class. This type of defense and restraint has been used in many job applications such as security, law enforcement, school teachers, EMT, and human service

     Ebook Item#: NSDSE $11.99

     Paperback item#: NSDSP $15.49

     Pack of 10 item# NSDSP10 $100

Officials Training For Combat Sports

This book covers Self-Defense, rules for continuous point sparing, team sparring, Muay Thai, and MMA. This is being used to train officials and *security personnel*[1]. This would also be a good program for law enforcement, teachers, security for any *programs*[2] including sports or people working with troubled youth. As well as an addition to a martial arts class

     Ebook Item#: OTCS $11.99

     Paper Back Item#: OTCSP $15.49

     10 Pack Item# OTCSP10 $100

---

1.   *http://www.wrkf.us/BookandCD.htm*

2.   *http://www.wrkf.us/BookandCD.htm*

Stretching By Scott Bolinger

This book covers Stretching Exercises that will limber up the upper and lower body. This takes you through a full stretching routine.

Ebook Item# WRSEB: $7.99
   Paperback WRSPB: $12.49
   Pack of 10 Item# WRS10: $100

Weight Lifting
by
Scott Bolinger

The author has trained in boxing, karate, weight training with his father Larry Bolinger (former Mr.Nebraska). This book shows many of the different weight lifting exercises and then has several weight lifting routines to follow. There are routines for full-body routines that can be done every other day, and there are routines

Ebook Item#: WRW $7.99

Paper Back Item#: WRWP $12.49

10 Pack Item#: WRW10 $100

Property Management by Scott Bolinger (2nd Edition)

This book covers a diverse property management business. It goes through Property Preservation and lists a few of the national companies that you can seek to contract with. This line of work is on foreclosed properties. The book also goes through house inspections and how to create a business doing house inspections or property preservation, as well as being a landlord and the does and don'ts. There is also a chapter on forms, for both standard forms for business and forms to be kept for taxes.

Ebook Item #102PM: $14.49

CD Item #102PM CD: $14.49

Paperback Book item #: 102PM: $25

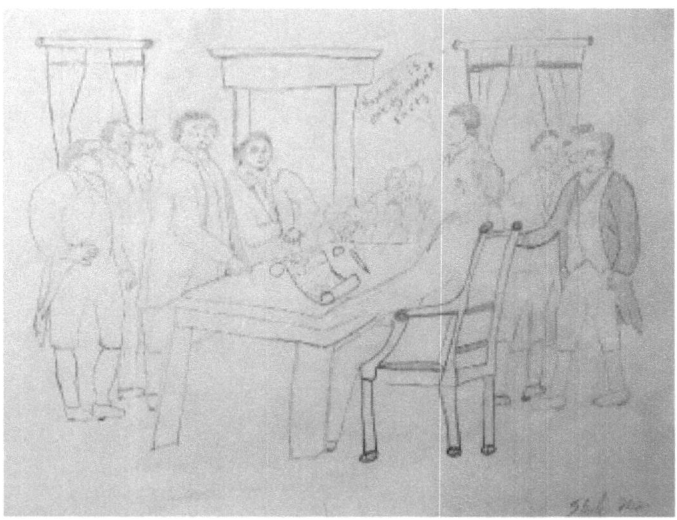

www.LarryBolinger.com[3]

Politics: Last Act of Defiance: This book was started based on my fight against a corrupt government. I served on a community board and ran for several public offices. The local city government and city council did not like my campaigns so I became a political target. I took a lot of heat from the local government for several years. They interfered with my business and my everyday life. I had to put up with their misinformation and defamatory campaigns. After a couple of years of being attacked regularly, I decided that I should start recording every encounter. A couple of encounters is not a big deal. 50 encounters start to become a big deal. So I started collecting all documents to prepare for a possible suit against the city. After several years of taking heat and the government's refusal to let up, I figure they were not going to go away. The local government made me a political target which destroyed both my reputation and business. I had put up with the city creating misinformation about me and my business. I was harassed, segregated, and ostracized and they put me in a position that forced me to consider packing up and moving out of town or to fight back. This book goes through many of the battles I went through. It also goes through many

---

3.   http://www.LarryBolinger.com

of the policies that I have sent to local, state, and federal lawmakers to help promote change. I also go through several research analyses that I had conducted. I hope that this book will help serve as inspiration for people to keep fighting and if that doesn't work, then fight smart.

Ebook #LAD-E: $10
CD book # LAD-CD: $12.89
Ebook: $10
Paperback: $25

For more information on Scott Bolinger books, CDs, ebooks, kindle books, you can go to the website www.WarriorRage.com[4], www.LarryBolinger.com[5] or email: LB@LarryBolinger.com.
Published by:
Scott Bolinger
Address: 507 Niobrara
Alliance, NE 69301
Phone: 308-760-7346 Email: LB@LarryBolinger.com
Website: www.WarriorRage.com
Revised 2016
Revised 2022

---

4. http://www.WarriorRage.com

5. http://www.LarryBolinger.com

Don't miss out!

Visit the website below and you can sign up to receive emails whenever Scott Bolinger publishes a new book. There's no charge and no obligation.

https://books2read.com/r/B-A-MTJL-WLCHB

BOOKS 2 READ

Connecting independent readers to independent writers.

Also by Scott Bolinger

1 of 3
Boxing Basics Level 1

2 of 3
Boxing Basics Level 2

3 of 3
Boxing Basic 3 & 4

Masters Edition
WarriorRage KickBoxing

Volume I
WarriorRage KickBoxing

Volume II
WarriorRage KickBoxing

Standalone
Officials Training Book for Combat Sports
Weight Lifting
Stretching by Scott Bolinger
National Self-Defense Solutions
Property Management by Scott Bolinger
Bolinger KickBoxing
Politics: Last Act of Defiance

Watch for more at larrybolinger.com/index.html.